Thank You

Dear Parents and Teachers,

We extend our heartfelt gratitude to each of you for choosing our Science of Reading curriculum. Your decision to invest in your child's education is commendable, and we are honored to be a part of their reading journey. At the heart of our curriculum lies the fundamental understanding of phonemic awareness, phonics, and the integration of decodable books, all of which are pivotal in fostering strong literacy skills in young readers. Phonemic awareness forms the basis of understanding how sounds work in words, while phonics provides the essential link between sounds and letters, empowering children to decode words with confidence.

We firmly believe that this curriculum serves as the crucial first step in your child's reading journey, laying down a solid foundation upon which further literacy skills can be built. The incorporation of decodable books ensures that children have access to texts that align closely with the phonics principles they are learning, facilitating a seamless transition from decoding to comprehension. As your child embarks on this exciting adventure of learning to read, rest assured that our curriculum is designed to support their growth every step of the way.

Should you have any questions or require further assistance regarding the curriculum or your child's progress, please do not hesitate to reach out to us at decodabletexts@gmail.com. We are here to support you and your child on this enriching journey towards literacy mastery. Once again, thank you for choosing our Science of Reading curriculum. Together, we can unlock the transformative power of reading in your child's life.

Warm regards,
Adam Free

TABLE OF CONTENTS

TABLE OF CONTENTS

Lesson Format

Each lesson will follow the following format. The total length of the lesson should last around thirty minutes. The format and the time breakdown can be seen below.

1. Phonemic awareness (hear it, 5 min)
   a. Isolating.
   b. Blending.
   c. Segmenting.
2. Word and sentence reading (decode it, 5 min)
   a. Read words with the target sound.
   b. Read sentences with the target sound.
3. Decodable book read (read it, 15 min)
   a. Read a decodable text with the target sound.
   b. Reading comprehension (Optional).
   c. Silly sentences.
4. Phonics activities (spell it 5 min)
   a. Spell words with the target sound pattern.
   b. Sound manipulation.

Definitions

- **Phonemic awareness**– Phonemic awareness is the ability to hear and work with the different sounds in spoken words. For example, it's knowing that the word "cat" is made up of the sounds c-a-t, and being able to play around with these sounds.

- **Segmenting–** Segmenting is breaking a word down into its individual sounds. For example, taking the word "dog" and splitting it into its sounds: d-o-g. This helps children learn to read and spell by understanding how different sounds come together to form words.

- **Blending**– Blending is the process of combining individual sounds to form a word. For example, when you hear the sounds b-l-a-ck and put them together to make the word "black."

Definitions

- **Isolating-** Isolating is the ability to pick out a single sound from a word. For example, in the word "sun," isolating the first sound would be hearing the "s" sound on its own.
- **Reading Comprehension Using the 5W's-** For this reading comprehension exercise, students will use the five W's to retell the story. The 5 W's are:
  - Who- Who is the main character or characters?
  - What- what did the main character do?
  - When- When did the story take place?
  - Where- Where did the story take place?
  - Why- Why did the events in the story take place?

Example Script- Isolating

Greet the students and explain the activity: "Today, we're going to play a listening game! We'll listen to some words and figure out what sound each word starts with. All the words we'll use have a short 'a' sound like in 'apple'."

Warm-Up:
- Say the word "cat" slowly and clearly. You can also segment it to model how to get the first sound (c-a-t). Then ask, "What is the first sound you hear in 'cat'?"
- Let the student respond, then confirm, "Yes, it starts with the 'c' sound, which sounds like 'cuh'."

Guided Practice:
- Introduce the next word by saying it clearly: "Listen carefully, 'mat'. What's the first sound in 'mat'?" Again, encourage students to segment the word, especially if they are having trouble (m-a-t).
- Continue with each word in the list.

Example Script- Blending

Greet the students and explain the activity: "Today we're going to play another fun listening game. We will listen to some sounds and put them together to make words. All these words will have the short 'a' sound in the middle, like in 'apple'."

Warm-Up:
- Start by saying the sounds of a simple word slowly and separately. For example, "Listen to these sounds: /c/ /a/ /t/. When we put these sounds together, they make the word 'cat'. Let's say them faster together. C-a-t, Cat. Can you try?"
- Guide the student to say the sounds separately and then blend them to form the word.

Guided Practice:
- Proceed with the next set of sounds. Say, "/m/ /a/ /t/," and then ask, "What word do these sounds make when we put them together?"
- Encourage the student to blend the sounds into the word "mat." Provide feedback as needed.
- Repeat the process with the rest of the words.

Example Script- Segmenting

Greet the students and explain the activity: "Today, we're going to play a sound detective game. We'll take words apart and find out what sounds are in them. All the words we'll use today have a short 'a' sound like in 'hat'."

Warm-Up:
- Start with a simple word. Say, "Let's take the word 'cat'. When we slow it down, we can hear all the sounds that make it up. Listen: 'cat' - /c/ /a/ /t/. Can you say the sounds with me?"
- Have the student repeat the sounds after you, emphasizing each sound.

Guided Practice:
- Introduce the next word, such as "mat." Say, "Now, let's try with 'mat'. What sounds do you hear in 'mat'?"
- Let the student attempt to break the word into sounds. Confirm and correct gently as needed, helping them focus on each distinct sound: /m/ /a/ /t/.
- Continue with more words.

Long A Vowel
Team- ai
Set 1

Hear it

Isolating

Ask your student to isolate the **beginning** sound in each word. Do not allow them to see the words or the book. This is an oral exercise.

- **Rain**
- **Plain**
- **Paint**
- **Chain**
- **Stain**
- **Drain**

Ask your student to isolate the **middle** sound in each word. Do not allow them to see the words or the book. This is an oral exercise.

- **Brain**
- **Claim**
- **Flail**
- **Bran**
- **Clam**
- **Fall**

Hear it

Isolating

Ask your student to isolate the **last** sound in each word. Do not allow them to see the words or the book. This is an oral exercise.

- **Maid**
- **Sail**
- **Snail**
- **Trail**
- **Waist**
- **Braid**

Blending

Ask your student to blend the following sounds into words.

- **D-r-ai-n**
- **B-r-ai-n**
- **C-l-ai-m**
- **P-l-ai-n**
- **P-ai-n-t**
- **Ch-ai-n**

Hear it

Segmenting

Ask your student to break apart the
following words into sounds.

- **Train**
- **Pail**
- **Quail**

- **Fairy**
- **Faint**
- **Spain**

Rhyming

Read the pair of words. If the two words
rhyme, ask students to put a thumb up. If
they do not rhyme, ask them to put a thumb
down.

- **Brain**   **Grain**
- **Drain**   **Rain**
- **Spain**   **Spine**

Decode it

Word Reading

Ask your student to read the following words.

- **Frail**
- **Grain**
- **Mail**
- **Maid**
- **Sail**
- **Snail**

Sentence Reading

Ask your student to read the following sentences.

- **The snail left a trail.**
- **Paint the chair blue.**
- **The train is late.**
- **She has a frail dog.**

4

Read it

A snail is in the rain. It trails on the wet path. The rain hits the snail's shell. A big snail joins the trail. They claim a dry spot. The snails wait and chat. Rain fades, and the sun sails high. The trail shines bright. The snails slide to the grass. They stay safe, side by side, in the shade.

READ IT—THE 5 W'S (OPTIONAL)

Name: _____

Date: _____

Who?	
What?	
When?	
Where?	
Why?	

Read it
Silly Sentences

Ask your student to read the following nonsense words from the box below. Though these are not real words, the goal is to get students to read them fluently and quickly. To accomplish this, you student may try as many times as possible within 3-5 minutes.

1. **The craim played with a blait.**
2. **A bairs ate the crait.**
3. **The fraip has a zait hat.**
4. **Waibs like to flaim.**
5. **The jain hops on the vait**

Spell it

Ask your student to spell and write the following words: Mail, Maid, Sail, Pail, Rain.

___ ___ ___ ___

___ ___ ___ ___

___ ___ ___ ___

___ ___ ___ ___

___ ___ ___ ___

Spell it
Word Ladder

Find the word at the bottom of the ladder.
Ask your student to change a few letters to make a new word.
For example, "Late" can be changed into "Fate" but changing the
first letter. Ask your student to do this until they run out of
words or complete the ladder.

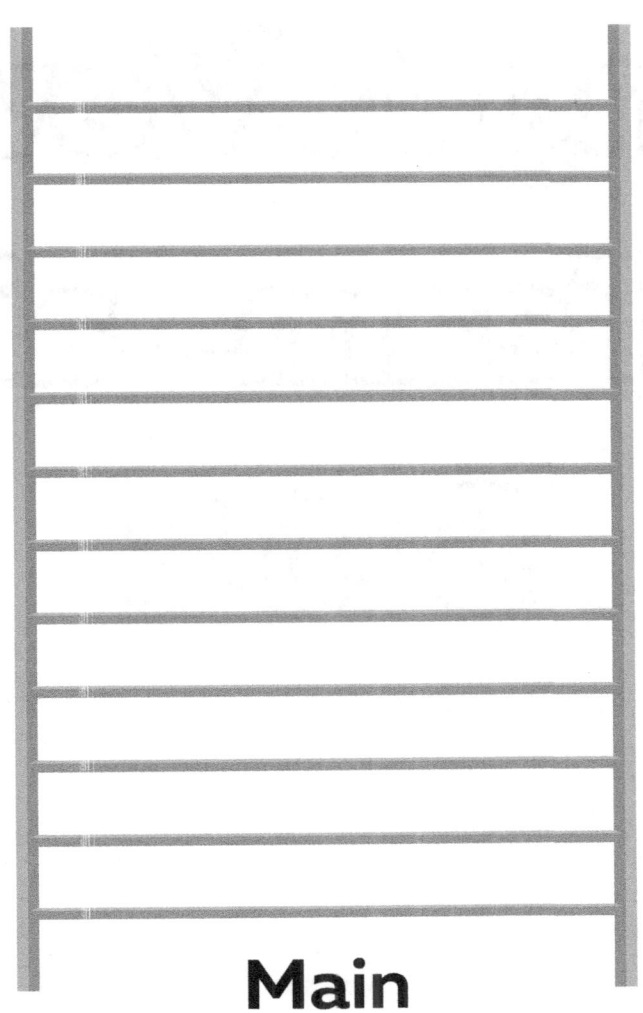

Main

Long A Vowel
Team- ai
Set 2

Hear it

Isolating

Ask your student to isolate the **beginning** sound in each word. Do not allow them to see the words or the book. This is an oral exercise.

- **Bait**
- **Fail**
- **Maid**
- **Vain**
- **Rain**
- **Sail**

Ask your student to isolate the **middle** sound in each word. Do not allow them to see the words or the book. This is an oral exercise.

- **Brain**
- **Fade**
- **Pain**
- **Brand**
- **Fad**
- **Pan**

Hear it

Isolating

Ask your student to isolate the **last** sound in each word. Do not allow them to see the words or the book. This is an oral exercise.

- **Hail**
- **Wail**
- **Laid**
- **Pain**
- **Stain**
- **Trail**

Blending

Ask your student to blend the following sounds into words.

- **P-ai-r**
- **F-ai-l**
- **J-ai-l**
- **L-ai-r**
- **G-ai-n**
- **F-ai-r**

Hear it

Segmenting

Ask your student to break apart the following words into sounds.

- **Grain**
- **Brain**
- **Claim**
- **Drain**
- **Paint**
- **Plain**

Rhyming

Read the pair of words. If the two words rhyme, ask students to put a thumb up. If they do not rhyme, ask them to put a thumb down.

- **Lair**   **Fair**
- **Claim**   **Clam**
- **Fail**   **Jail**

Decode it

Word Reading

Ask your student to read the following words.

- **Nail**
- **Pair**
- **Lair**
- **Fair**
- **Gain**
- **Hail**

Sentence Reading

Ask your student to read the following sentences.

- **The maid will wait.**
- **He set a trap with bait.**
- **The pair of quails ran.**
- **I will mail the grain.**

Read it

A quail waits in the rain. It spots a snail on the trail. The quail pecks at the grain on the ground. A train passes by and the quail flaps its wings. The rain stops, and the quail sees a fair sky. It hops to a dry spot and preens its tail. The quail stays safe, calm and still.

READ IT—THE 5 W'S (OPTIONAL)

Name: _____

Date: _____

Who?	
What?	
When?	
Where?	
Why?	

Read it
Silly Sentences

Ask your student to read the following nonsense words from the box below. Though these are not real words, the goal is to get students to read them fluently and quickly. To accomplish this, you student may try as many times as possible within 3-5 minutes.

1. **The baip dain on a vail.**
2. **Zail the grait to flain.**
3. **Frait the laig of a mair.**
4. **Kaint the jair with naid.**
5. **Kail the craid with a saip.**

Spell it

Ask your student to spell and write the following words: Fair, Lair, Vain, Rail, Sail

_____ _____ _____ _____

_____ _____ _____ _____

_____ _____ _____ _____

_____ _____ _____ _____

_____ _____ _____ _____

Spell it
Word Ladder

Find the word at the bottom of the ladder.
Ask your student to change a few letters to make a new word.
For example, "Late" can be changed into "Fate" but changing the
first letter. Ask your student to do this until they run out of
words or complete the ladder.

Lair

Long A Vowel
Team- ai
Set 3

Hear it

Isolating

Ask your student to isolate the **beginning** sound in each word. Do not allow them to see the words or the book. This is an oral exercise.

- **Plain**
- **Chain**
- **Quail**
- **Frail**
- **Mail**
- **Snail**

Ask your student to isolate the **middle** sound in each word. Do not allow them to see the words or the book. This is an oral exercise.

- **Braid**
- **Flail**
- **Waist**
- **Brad**
- **Flan**
- **Watch**

Hear it

Isolating

Ask your student to isolate the **last** sound in each word. Do not allow them to see the words or the book. This is an oral exercise.

- **Brain**
- **Grain**
- **Claim**
- **Paint**
- **Drain**
- **Plain**

Blending

Ask your student to blend the following sounds into words.

- **R-ai-l**
- **B-r-ai-n**
- **Ch-ai-n**
- **G-r-ai-n**
- **D-r-ai-n**
- **P-l-ai-n**

Hear it

Segmenting

Ask your student to break apart the following words into sounds.

- **Saint**
- **Snail**
- **Stair**
- **Trail**
- **Waist**
- **Maid**

Rhyming

Read the pair of words. If the two words rhyme, ask students to put a thumb up. If they do not rhyme, ask them to put a thumb down.

- **Brain**   **Drain**
- **Tail**   **Tale**
- **Lair**   **Land**

Decode it

Word Reading

Ask your student to read the following words.

- **Braid**
- **Flail**
- **Waist**
- **Grain**
- **Paint**
- **Plain**

Sentence Reading

Ask your student to read the following sentences.

- **The snail is on the trail.**
- **Paint the plain chair.**
- **The train is fast.**
- **She will mail the letter.**

Read it

A maid named Gail had a task. She had to paint a plain wall. Gail got a pail of paint. She did not fail. The paint was bright and fair. A snail came in from the rain. Gail made it a small trail. The snail was glad. Gail's job was done. She had a smile. The wall was great!

READ IT—THE 5 W'S (OPTIONAL)

Name: _____

Date: _____

Who?	
What?	
When?	
Where?	
Why?	

Read it
Silly Sentences

Ask your student to read the following nonsense words from the box below. Though these are not real words, the goal is to get students to read them fluently and quickly. To accomplish this, you student may try as many times as possible within 3-5 minutes.

1. **The frait zail in the cair.**
2. **Daint the craip with maib.**
3. **Flain the jair for a baid.**
4. **Kaint the vait on the slaid.**
5. **The waip met a kail.**

Spell it

Ask your student to spell and write the following words: Grain, Drain, Brain, Train, Chain

Spell it
Word Ladder

Find the word at the bottom of the ladder.
Ask your student to change a few letters to make a new word.
For example, "Late" can be changed into "Fate" but changing the
first letter. Ask your student to do this until they run out of
words or complete the ladder.

Chain

Long A Vowel Team- ay and ey Set 1

Hear it

Isolating

Ask your student to isolate the **beginning** sound in each word. Do not allow them to see the words or the book. This is an oral exercise.

- **Stay**
- **Play**
- **Gray**
- **Tray**
- **Obey**
- **Prey**

Ask your student to isolate the **middle** sound in each word. Do not allow them to see the words or the book. This is an oral exercise.

- **Array**
- **Sway**
- **Inlay**
- **Away**
- **Then**
- **Grand**

Hear it

Isolating

Ask your student to isolate the **last** sound in each word. Do not allow them to see the words or the book. This is an oral exercise.

- **Day**
- **Gram**
- **Grey**
- **Sunk**
- **Bat**
- **Maps**

Blending

Ask your student to blend the following sounds into words.

- **S-ay**
- **H-ey**
- **B-ay**
- **P-r-ey**
- **T-r-ay**
- **C-l-ay**

Hear it

Segmenting

Ask your student to break apart the following words into sounds.

- **Slay**
- **Play**
- **Clay**
- **Lay**
- **Day**
- **Prey**

Rhyming

Read the pair of words. If the two words rhyme, ask students to put a thumb up. If they do not rhyme, ask them to put a thumb down.

- **Pray**   **Prey**
- **Bay**   **Say**
- **Tray**   **Tram**

Decode it

Word Reading

Ask your student to read the following words.

- **Stay**
- **Play**
- **Obey**
- **Prey**
- **Hey**
- **Gray**

Sentence Reading

Ask your student to read the following sentences.

- **The gray cat will play.**
- **They say to obey rules.**
- **She found a tray today.**
- **The tray is on the table.**

Read it

A boy has a spray can. He likes to spray paint. The spray is bright and fun. One day, he saw a grey wall. He said, "Hey, I will spray this wall!" He made a big sun with his spray. People saw the sun and said, "Hey, that's nice!" The boy felt happy. He put the spray can away and went to play.

READ IT—THE 5 W'S (OPTIONAL)

Name: _____

Date: _____

Who?	
What?	
When?	
Where?	
Why?	

Read it
Silly Sentences

Ask your student to read the following nonsense words from the box below. Though these are not real words, the goal is to get students to read them fluently and quickly. To accomplish this, you student may try as many times as possible within 3-5 minutes.

1. **The Trey fleys on a kay.**
2. **Zey the qay with a pley.**
3. **Fay and dey pley in the bey.**
4. **The smay eats a trey.**
5. **Wey and tey vray the glay**

Spell it

Ask your student to spell and write the following words: Tray, Pray, Slay, Prey, Obey.

_____ _____ _____ _____

_____ _____ _____ _____

_____ _____ _____ _____

_____ _____ _____ _____

_____ _____ _____ _____

35

Spell it
Word Ladder

Find the word at the bottom of the ladder.
Ask your student to change a few letters to make a new word.
For example, "Late" can be changed into "Fate" but changing the
first letter. Ask your student to do this until they run out of
words or complete the ladder.

Tray

Spell it
Word Ladder

Find the word at the bottom of the ladder.
Ask your student to change a few letters to make a new word.
For example, "Late" can be changed into "Fate" but changing the
first letter. Ask your student to do this until they run out of
words or complete the ladder.

Hey

Long A Vowel Team- ay and ey Set 2

Hear it

Isolating

Ask your student to isolate the **beginning** sound in each word. Do not allow them to see the words or the book. This is an oral exercise.

- **Play**
- **Me**
- **Tray**
- **Key**
- **Them**
- **Grunt**

Ask your student to isolate the **middle** sound in each word. Do not allow them to see the words or the book. This is an oral exercise.

- **Obey**
- **Away**
- **Hey**
- **Check**
- **Clay**
- **Pray**

Hear it

Isolating

Ask your student to isolate the **last** sound in each word. Do not allow them to see the words or the book. This is an oral exercise.

- **Maybe**
- **Brays**
- **Layout**
- **Delay**
- **Payoff**
- **Always**

Blending

Ask your student to blend the following sounds into words.

- **D-e-l-a-y**
- **S-w-a-y**
- **S-t-a-y**
- **A-ll-e-y**
- **P-r-e-y**
- **Th-e-y**

Hear it
Segmenting

Ask your student to break apart the following words into sounds.

- **Say**
- **They**
- **Midway**
- **Away**
- **Stay**
- **Saying**

Rhyming

Read the pair of words. If the two words rhyme, ask students to put a thumb up. If they do not rhyme, ask them to put a thumb down.

- **Tray**   **Try**
- **Day**   **Lay**
- **Gray**   **Grey**

Decode it

Word Reading

Ask your student to read the following words.

- **Away**
- **Prey**
- **Hey**
- **Midday**
- **Play**
- **Dismay**

Sentence Reading

Ask your student to read the following sentences.

- **The tray holds hay.**
- **They will stay here.**
- **Pay the fee today.**
- **The prey is near.**

Read it

A boy saw a key in the hay midday. He said, "Hey, what is this?" The key was gray and old. He ran to show his mom. She said, "This key may open a box." They went to the shed to find the box. The boy used the key, and it fit! The boy was happy and went to play.

READ IT—THE 5 W'S (OPTIONAL)

Name: _____

Date: _____

Who?	
What?	
When?	
Where?	
Why?	

Read it

Silly Sentences

Ask your student to read the following nonsense words from the box below. Though these are not real words, the goal is to get students to read them fluently and quickly. To accomplish this, you student may try as many times as possible within 3-5 minutes.

1. The vray fleys in the qay.
2. Zey the zay with a smay.
3. Wey and dey krey in the bey.
4. The kay met a flay.
5. Vey the jey is a ley.

Spell it

Ask your student to spell and write the following words: Jay, Midway, Play, Sway, Days.

--- --- ---

--- --- --- --- ---

--- --- --- ---

--- --- --- ---

--- --- --- ---

Spell it
Word Ladder

Find the word at the bottom of the ladder.
Ask your student to change a few letters to make a new word.
For example, "Late" can be changed into "Fate" but changing the
first letter. Ask your student to do this until they run out of
words or complete the ladder.

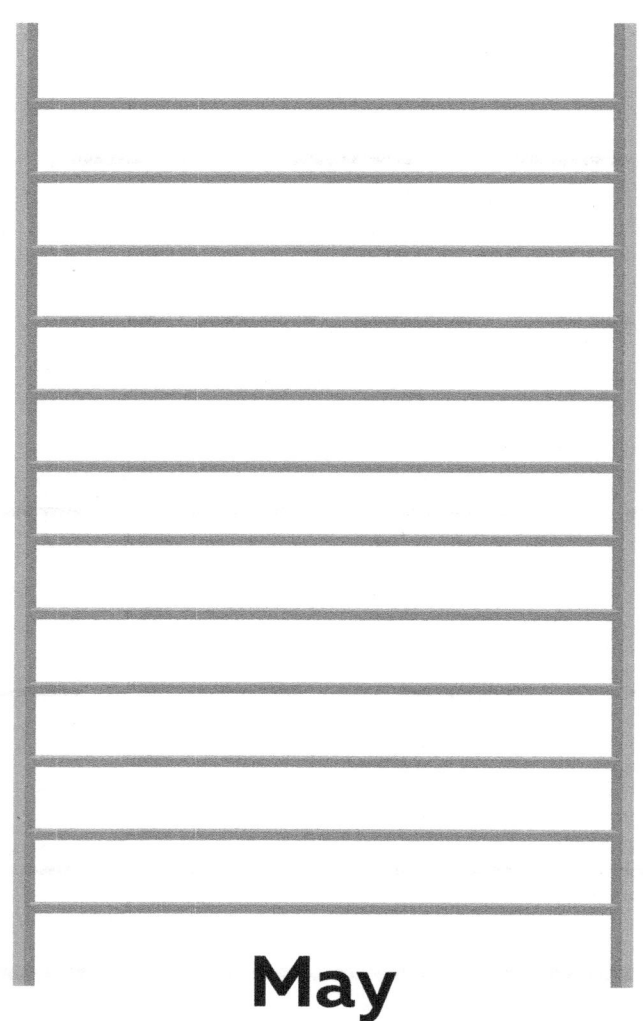

May

Spell it
Word Ladder

Find the word at the bottom of the ladder.
Ask your student to change a few letters to make a new word.
For example, "Late" can be changed into "Fate" but changing the
first letter. Ask your student to do this until they run out of
words or complete the ladder.

They

Long A Vowel Team- ea, ei, and eigh Set 1

Hear it

Isolating

Ask your student to isolate the **beginning** sound in each word. Do not allow them to see the words or the book. This is an oral exercise.

- **Steak**
- **Break**
- **Great**
- **Eight**
- **Weigh**
- **Vein**

Ask your student to isolate the **middle** sound in each word. Do not allow them to see the words or the book. This is an oral exercise.

- **Eight**
- **Vein**
- **Weigh**
- **Team**
- **When**
- **Great**

Hear it

Isolating

Ask your student to isolate the **last** sound in each word. Do not allow them to see the words or the book. This is an oral exercise.

- **Breakup**
- **Break**
- **Steak**
- **Swim**
- **Weigh**
- **Dream**

Blending

Ask your student to blend the following sounds into words.

- **G-r-ea-t**
- **R-ei-n**
- **V-ei-n**
- **W-eigh**
- **Eigh-t**
- **B-r-ea-k**

Hear it

Segmenting

Ask your student to break apart the following words into sounds.

- **Steak**
- **Vein**
- **Tear**
- **Eight**
- **Weigh**
- **Reign**

Rhyming

Read the pair of words. If the two words rhyme, ask students to put a thumb up. If they do not rhyme, ask them to put a thumb down.

- **Steak**   **Rake**
- **Wear**   **Were**
- **Neigh**   **Near**

Decode it

Word Reading

Ask your student to read the following words.

- **Reign**
- **Break**
- **Outbreak**
- **Weigh**
- **Eight**
- **Eighty**

Sentence Reading

Ask your student to read the following sentences.

- **She will weigh the beans.**
- **The tear was hard to see.**
- **Eight birds flew by.**
- **He will clean the sleigh.**

Read it

A man had a big steak. He put it on the grill to cook. The heat made it great. He used a fork to turn the steak. He had to weigh it first. The steak was thick and good. He cut it into eight pieces to share. The grill had some wear and tear, but it still worked well. They all enjoyed the tasty steak.

READ IT—THE 5 W'S (OPTIONAL)

Name: _____

Date: _____

Who?	
What?	
When?	
Where?	
Why?	

Read it
Silly Sentences

Ask your student to read the following nonsense words from the box below. Though these are not real words, the goal is to get students to read them fluently and quickly. To accomplish this, you student may try as many times as possible within 3-5 minutes.

1. **The veigh veighs in the neak.**
2. **Leat the beap with greigh.**
3. **Heigh the teap on the reat.**
4. **Meak the dreigh in the fleat.**
5. **Feigh the zeap with skea**

Spell it

Ask your student to spell and write the following words: Rein, Vein, Pear, Eight, Steak.

_____ _____ _____ _____

_____ _____ _____ _____

_____ _____ _____ _____

_ _ _ _ _ _ _ _

_ _ _ _ _ _ _ _

Spell it
Word Ladder

Find the word at the bottom of the ladder.
Ask your student to change a few letters to make a new word.
For example, "Late" can be changed into "Fate" but changing the
first letter. Ask your student to do this until they run out of
words or complete the ladder.

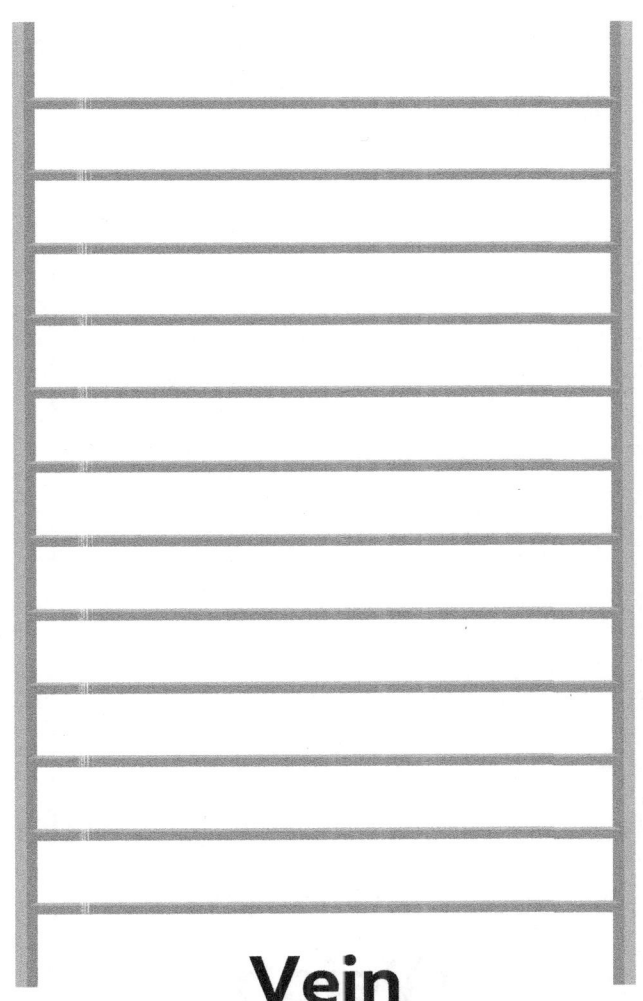

Vein

Spell it
Word Ladder

Find the word at the bottom of the ladder.
Ask your student to change a few letters to make a new word.
For example, "Late" can be changed into "Fate" but changing the
first letter. Ask your student to do this until they run out of
words or complete the ladder.

Weigh

Long A Vowel Team- ea, ei, and eigh Set 2

Hear it

Isolating

Ask your student to isolate the **beginning** sound in each word. Do not allow them to see the words or the book. This is an oral exercise.

- **Eight**
- **Ben**
- **Weigh**
- **Tear**
- **When**
- **Bat**

Ask your student to isolate the **middle** sound in each word. Do not allow them to see the words or the book. This is an oral exercise.

- **Eighty**
- **Rein**
- **Weight**
- **Beige**
- **Weight**
- **Freight**

Hear it

Isolating

Ask your student to isolate the **last** sound in each word. Do not allow them to see the words or the book. This is an oral exercise.

- **Sweat**
- **Break**
- **Steak**
- **Tear**
- **Weight**
- **Neighbor**

Blending

Ask your student to blend the following sounds into words.

- **Eigh-t**
- **B-ei-ge**
- **V-ei-n**
- **N-eigh**
- **W-eigh-t**
- **S-t-ea-k**

Hear it

Segmenting

Ask your student to break apart the following words into sounds.

- **Vein**
- **Veil**
- **Sleigh**
- **Weigh**
- **Eight**
- **Neigh**

Rhyming

Read the pair of words. If the two words rhyme, ask students to put a thumb up. If they do not rhyme, ask them to put a thumb down.

- **Pear**   **Pair**
- **Eight**   **Ate**
- **Freight**   **Were**

Decode it
Word Reading

Ask your student to read the following words.

- **Eight**
- **Neigh**
- **Weigh**
- **Veil**
- **Pear**
- **Great**

Sentence Reading

Ask your student to read the following sentences.

- **She will weigh the beans.**
- **He will wear eight the shirts today.**
- **They will clean the sleigh.**

Read it

A girl had a ripe pear. She took a bite and felt a vein in her hand. The pear was great. She counted eight seeds inside. She wanted to share the pear with eighty girls. But she would need a freight to carry all of the weight. So the girl had to breakup with the idea.

READ IT-THE 5 W'S (OPTIONAL)

Name: _____

Date: _____

Who?	
What?	
When?	
Where?	
Why?	

Read it
Silly Sentences

Ask your student to read the following nonsense words from the box below. Though these are not real words, the goal is to get students to read them fluently and quickly. To accomplish this, you student may try as many times as possible within 3-5 minutes.

1. **The tein veighs in the pein.**
2. **Reigh the reigh with steat.**
3. **Heigh the plein on the mein.**
4. **Seik the dreigh in the reigh.**
5. **breit the tein with seit.**

Spell it

Ask your student to spell and write the following words: Vein, Rein, Eight, Great, Weight.

Spell it
Word Ladder

Find the word at the bottom of the ladder.
Ask your student to change a few letters to make a new word.
For example, "Late" can be changed into "Fate" but changing the
first letter. Ask your student to do this until they run out of
words or complete the ladder.

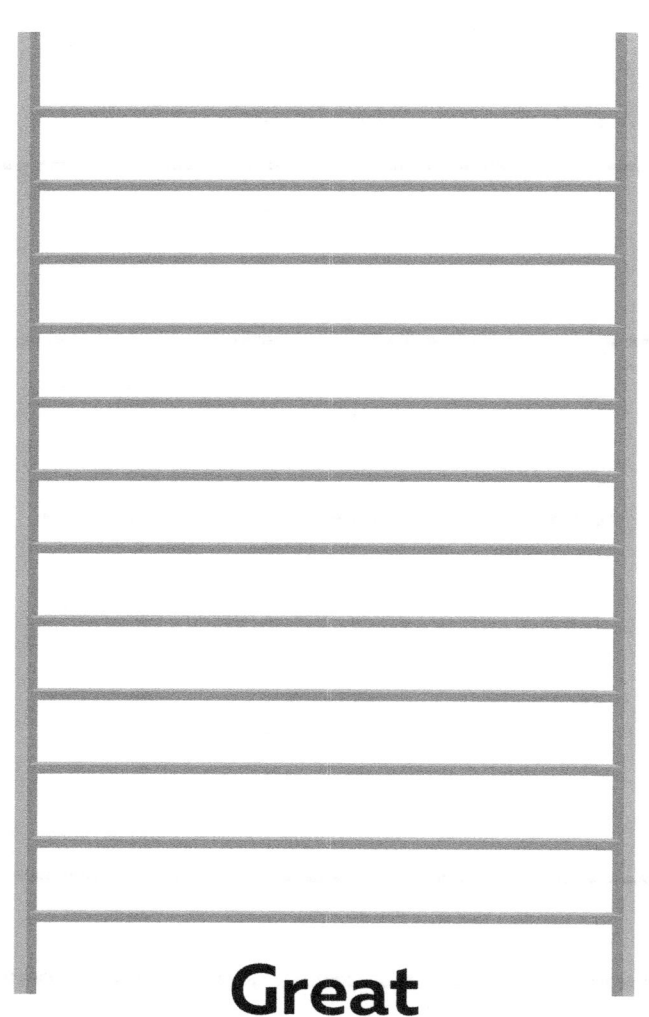

Great

Spell it
Word Ladder

Find the word at the bottom of the ladder.
Ask your student to change a few letters to make a new word.
For example, "Late" can be changed into "Fate" but changing the
first letter. Ask your student to do this until they run out of
words or complete the ladder.

Neigh

Long E Vowel Team- ea and ee Set 1

Hear it

Isolating

Ask your student to isolate the **beginning** sound in each word. Do not allow them to see the words or the book. This is an oral exercise.

- **Read**
- **Bead**
- **Lead**

- **Bee**
- **Fee**
- **See**

Ask your student to isolate the **middle** sound in each word. Do not allow them to see the words or the book. This is an oral exercise.

- **Ten**
- **Zen**
- **Flee**

- **Teal**
- **Zeal**
- **Flem**

Hear it

Isolating

Ask your student to isolate the **last** sound in each word. Do not allow them to see the words or the book. This is an oral exercise.

- **Plea**
- **Leaf**
- **Steal**
- **Freed**
- **Gleam**
- **Tree**

Blending

Ask your student to blend the following sounds into words.

- **P-l-ea**
- **F-l-ea**
- **D-ea-l**
- **S-ee**
- **Wh-ee-l**
- **T-ea-m**

Hear it

Segmenting

Ask your student to break apart the following words into sounds.

- **Deed**
- **Feed**
- **Heed**
- **Teal**
- **Meal**
- **Real**

Rhyming

Read the pair of words. If the two words rhyme, ask students to put a thumb up. If they do not rhyme, ask them to put a thumb down.

- **See**   **Mean**
- **Meal**   **Real**
- **When**   **Width**

Decode it
Word Reading

Ask your student to read the following words.

- **Bee**
- **Fee**
- **See**

- **Feet**
- **Weak**
- **Bean**

Sentence Reading

Ask your student to read the following sentences.

- **The sheep eat green grass.**
- **She will read and sleep.**
- **The sea is deep and clear.**
- **He feels the cool breeze.**

Read it

A bee buzzed by a green tree. It went to a red leaf. The bee saw sweet nectar to eat. It felt happy and free. The bee went near a stream and dipped to drink. The water was cool and clear. The bee then flew back to its hive. It made honey for the queen. The bee worked hard and felt good.

READ IT—THE 5 W'S (OPTIONAL)

Name: _____

Date: _____

Who?	
What?	
When?	
Where?	
Why?	

Read it
Silly Sentences

Ask your student to read the following nonsense words from the box below. Though these are not real words, the goal is to get students to read them fluently and quickly. To accomplish this, you student may try as many times as possible within 3-5 minutes.

1. **The teep is in the vleet.**
2. **Meep the teap on the zeek.**
3. **Xeak the leet with a zeel.**
4. **The neep eats a keap.**
5. **The dreek sees a meap.**

Spell it

Ask your student to spell and write the following words: Bean, Plea, Flea, Teen, Deed.

—	—	—	—
—	—	—	—
—	—	—	—
—	—	—	—
—	—	—	—

Spell it
Word Ladder

Find the word at the bottom of the ladder.
Ask your student to change a few letters to make a new word.
For example, "Late" can be changed into "Fate" but changing the
first letter. Ask your student to do this until they run out of
words or complete the ladder.

Bean

Spell it
Word Ladder

Find the word at the bottom of the ladder.
Ask your student to change a few letters to make a new word.
For example, "Late" can be changed into "Fate" but changing the
first letter. Ask your student to do this until they run out of
words or complete the ladder.

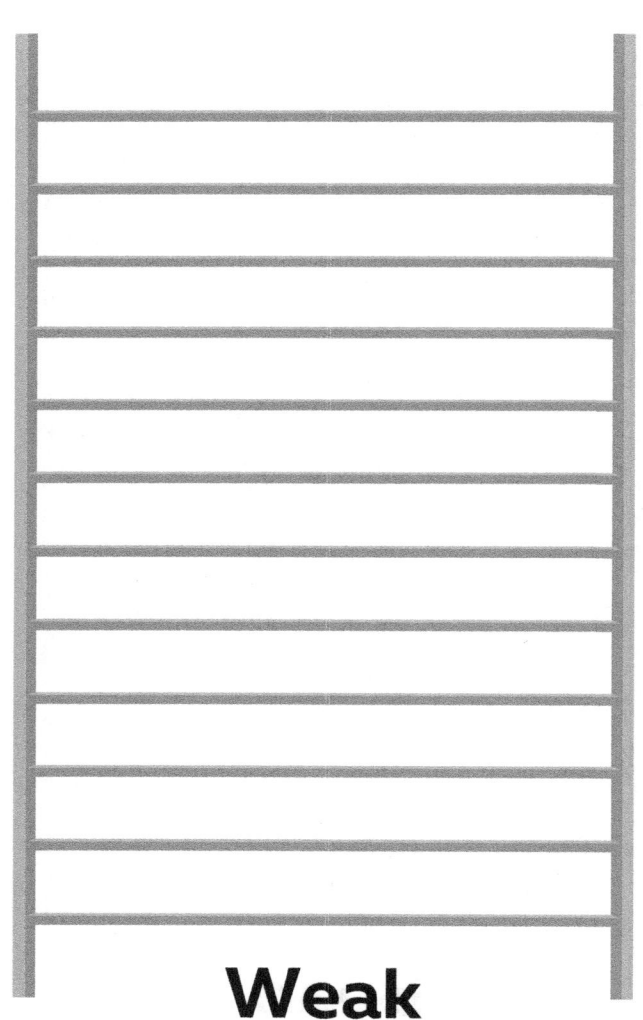

Weak

Long E Vowel Team- ea and ee Set 2

Hear it

Isolating

Ask your student to isolate the **beginning** sound in each word. Do not allow them to see the words or the book. This is an oral exercise.

- **Pea**
- **Sea**
- **Tea**
- **Need**
- **Reed**
- **Seed**

Ask your student to isolate the **middle** sound in each word. Do not allow them to see the words or the book. This is an oral exercise.

- **Ten**
- **Meek**
- **Peek**
- **Bead**
- **Lead**
- **Peck**

Hear it

Isolating

Ask your student to isolate the **last** sound in each word. Do not allow them to see the words or the book. This is an oral exercise.

- **Plead**
- **Beak**
- **Leak**
- **Week**
- **Cheek**
- **Creek**

Blending

Ask your student to blend the following sounds into words.

- **P-ea**
- **S-ea**
- **T-ea**
- **W-ee-d**
- **S-ee-d**
- **D-ee-d**

Hear it

Segmenting

Ask your student to break apart the following words into sounds.

- **Feel**
- **Heel**
- **Peel**
- **Deal**
- **Heal**
- **Meal**

Rhyming

Read the pair of words. If the two words rhyme, ask students to put a thumb up. If they do not rhyme, ask them to put a thumb down.

- **Feel**   **Peel**
- **Heel**   **Heal**
- **Meal**   **Mile**

Decode it

Word Reading

Ask your student to read the following words.

- **Sea**
- **Tea**
- **Weed**
- **Deed**
- **Seed**
- **Peel**

Sentence Reading

Ask your student to read the following sentences.

- **The team will meet soon.**
- **He feels the cool breeze.**
- **She wears a neat dress.**
- **We hear the bees buzz.**

Read it

A pea fell from the pod. It rolled near a green tree. A bee buzzed by and saw the pea. The bee flew to see the pea up close. The pea felt neat and cool. A sheep came to eat some grass. It saw the pea and sniffed it. The sheep did not eat the pea. The pea stayed near the tree, feeling free.

READ IT—THE 5 W'S (OPTIONAL)

Who?	
What?	
When?	
Where?	
Why?	

Read it
Silly Sentences

Ask your student to read the following nonsense words from the box below. Though these are not real words, the goal is to get students to read them fluently and quickly. To accomplish this, you student may try as many times as possible within 3-5 minutes.

1. **The zeap seels veet neek.**
2. **Meel the teep with a clee.**
3. **Geet the beap on the deek.**
4. **Leat the veep by the fead.**
5. **The keap sees a leet.**

Spell it

Ask your student to spell and write the following words: Need, Reed, Seed, Beak, Leak.

_____ _____ _____ _____

_____ _____ _____ _____

_____ _____ _____ _____

_____ _____ _____ _____

_____ _____ _____ _____

Spell it
Word Ladder

Find the word at the bottom of the ladder.
Ask your student to change a few letters to make a new word.
For example, "Late" can be changed into "Fate" but changing the
first letter. Ask your student to do this until they run out of
words or complete the ladder.

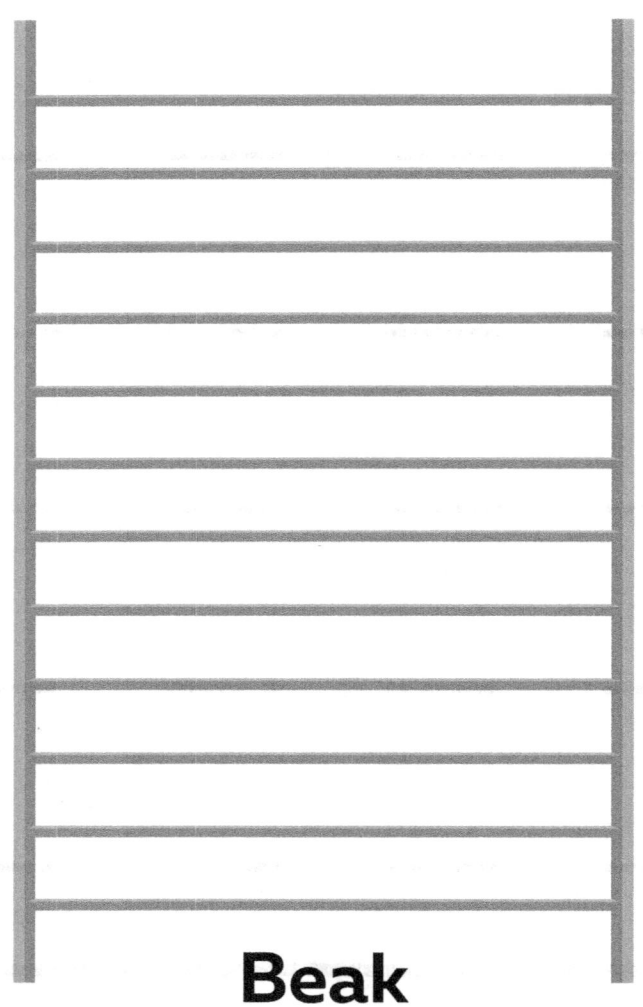

Beak

Spell it
Word Ladder

Find the word at the bottom of the ladder.
Ask your student to change a few letters to make a new word.
For example, "Late" can be changed into "Fate" but changing the
first letter. Ask your student to do this until they run out of
words or complete the ladder.

Seen

Long E Vowel Team- ea and ee Set 3

Hear it

Isolating

Ask your student to isolate the **beginning** sound in each word. Do not allow them to see the words or the book. This is an oral exercise.

- **Steel**
- **Keen**
- **Team**
- **Teen**
- **Beep**
- **Deep**

Ask your student to isolate the **middle** sound in each word. Do not allow them to see the words or the book. This is an oral exercise.

- **Feel**
- **Reef**
- **Ben**
- **Fell**
- **Ref**
- **Bean**

Hear it
Isolating

Ask your student to isolate the **last** sound in each word. Do not allow them to see the words or the book. This is an oral exercise.

- **Win**
- **Sheep**
- **Meat**
- **Heap**
- **Lean**
- **Meek**

Blending

Ask your student to blend the following sounds into words.

- **L-ea-n**
- **M-ea-n**
- **C-l-ea-n**
- **F-ee-l**
- **H-ee-l**
- **P-ee-l**

Hear it

Segmenting

Ask your student to break apart the following words into sounds.

- **Feel**
- **Heel**
- **Peel**
- **Deal**
- **Heal**
- **Meal**

Rhyming

Read the pair of words. If the two words rhyme, ask students to put a thumb up. If they do not rhyme, ask them to put a thumb down.

- **Steel**   **Meal**
- **Deer**   **Rear**
- **Seer**   **Seem**

Decode it

Word Reading

Ask your student to read the following words.

- **Weep**
- **Sheep**
- **Sleep**
- **Heap**
- **Leap**
- **Reap**

Sentence Reading

Ask your student to read the following sentences.

- **The deer leaps past the creek.**
- **She eats a peach by the sea.**
- **The queen sees her neat room.**
- **He feeds the sheep green leaves**

Read it

A sheep walks by the green tree. It sees a leaf and eats it. The sheep feels the cool breeze. It likes to be near the stream. The water is clear and neat. A bee buzzes by the sheep's ear. The sheep looks up and sees the blue sky. It is a calm day. The sheep lies down and falls asleep.

READ IT—THE 5 W'S (OPTIONAL)

Name: _____

Date: _____

Who?	
What?	
When?	
Where?	
Why?	

Read it
Silly Sentences

Ask your student to read the following nonsense words from the box below. Though these are not real words, the goal is to get students to read them fluently and quickly. To accomplish this, you student may try as many times as possible within 3-5 minutes.

1. The jeel eats a veap.
2. Meep the zeat on the greel.
3. Deel the feap to veep.
4. The neek zeets a deap.
5. Feek the leam with a keet

Spell it

Ask your student to spell and write the following words: Keen, Seen, Teen, Zeal, Leap.

_____ _____ _____ _____

_____ _____ _____ _____

_____ _____ _____ _____

_____ _____ _____ _____

_____ _____ _____ _____

Spell it
Word Ladder

Find the word at the bottom of the ladder.
Ask your student to change a few letters to make a new word.
For example, "Late" can be changed into "Fate" but changing the
first letter. Ask your student to do this until they run out of
words or complete the ladder.

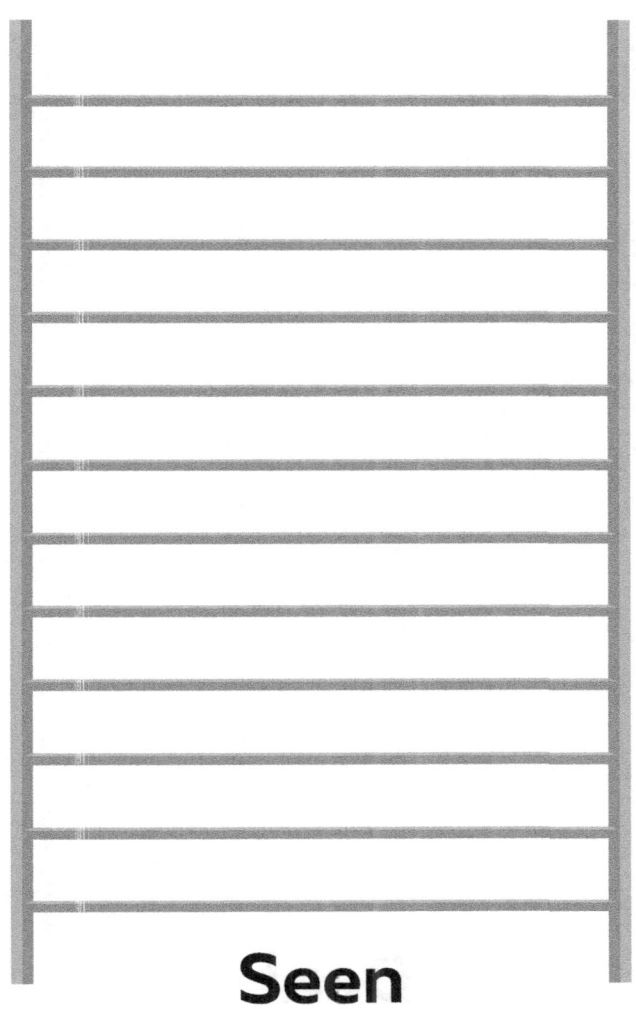

Seen

Spell it
Word Ladder

Find the word at the bottom of the ladder.
Ask your student to change a few letters to make a new word.
For example, "Late" can be changed into "Fate" but changing the
first letter. Ask your student to do this until they run out of
words or complete the ladder.

Deal

Long E Vowel Team-ey Set 1

Hear it

Isolating

Ask your student to isolate the **beginning** sound in each word. Do not allow them to see the words or the book. This is an oral exercise.

- **Key**
- **Alley**
- **Money**
- **Money**
- **Honey**
- **Valley**

Ask your student to isolate the **middle** sound in each word. Do not allow them to see the words or the book. This is an oral exercise.

- **Abbey**
- **Alley**
- **Honey**
- **Let**
- **Hat**
- **Gooey**

Hear it

Isolating

Ask your student to isolate the **last** sound in each word. Do not allow them to see the words or the book. This is an oral exercise.

- **Key**
- **Honey**
- **Lack**
- **Family**
- **Vast**
- **Abbey**

Blending

Ask your student to blend the following sounds into words.

- **K-ey**
- **H-o-n-ey**
- **A-ll-ey**
- **M-o-n-ey**
- **A-bb-ey**
- **K-ey**

Hear it

Segmenting

Ask your student to break apart the following words into sounds.

- **Abbey**
- **Alley**
- **Money**

- **Honey**
- **Key**
- **Honey**

Rhyming

Read the pair of words. If the two words rhyme, ask students to put a thumb up. If they do not rhyme, ask them to put a thumb down.

- **Honey**   **Money**
- **Key**   **Keen**
- **Alley**   **Abbey**

Decode it

Word Reading

Ask your student to read the following words.

- **Key**
- **Alley**
- **Abbey**
- **Money**
- **Honey**
- **Key**

Sentence Reading

Ask your student to read the following sentences.

- **The donkey walks to the honey.**
- **They play in the alley.**
- **The monkey is very funny.**
- **She found a key in the abbey.**

Read it

Tom found money in the alley. He picked it up and felt it was a key to happiness. He wanted to buy a monkey with the money. He went to the shop and saw a donkey. It was not what he wanted. But the donkey was cool. So he paid his money and took the donkey home. On the way to the abbey, he and the donkey saw a monkey. Tom, the monkey, and the donkey all went home.

READ IT-THE 5 W'S (OPTIONAL)

Name: _____

Date: _____

Who?	
What?	
When?	
Where?	
Why?	

Read it
Silly Sentences

Ask your student to read the following nonsense words from the box below. Though these are not real words, the goal is to get students to read them fluently and quickly. To accomplish this, you student may try as many times as possible within 3-5 minutes.

1. **The deys play in the tey.**
2. **Heey the brey with feey.**
3. **Mey the leys on the trey.**
4. **The reys see a wey.**
5. **Sey the peys to deey.**

Spell it

Ask your student to spell and write the following words: Key, Alley, Abbey, Money, Honey.

___ ___ ___

___ ___ ___ ___ ___

___ ___ ___ ___ ___

___ ___ ___ ___ ___

___ ___ ___ ___ ___

Spell it
Word Ladder

Find the word at the bottom of the ladder.
Ask your student to change a few letters to make a new word.
For example, "Late" can be changed into "Fate" but changing the
first letter. Ask your student to do this until they run out of
words or complete the ladder.

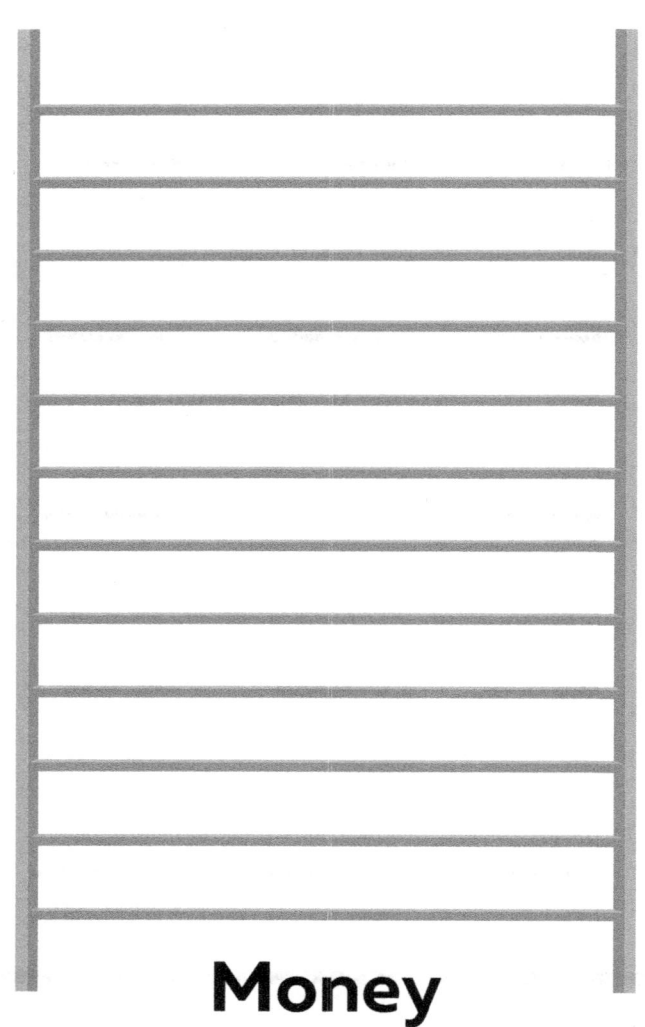

Money

Long E Vowel Team-ey Set 2

Hear it

Isolating

Ask your student to isolate the **beginning** sound in each word. Do not allow them to see the words or the book. This is an oral exercise.

- **Money**
- **Alley**
- **Honey**
- **Key**
- **Valley**
- **Abbey**

Ask your student to isolate the **middle** sound in each word. Do not allow them to see the words or the book. This is an oral exercise.

- **Keen**
- **Abbey**
- **Seat**
- **Lap**
- **Alley**
- **Set**

Hear it

Isolating

Ask your student to isolate the **last** sound in each word. Do not allow them to see the words or the book. This is an oral exercise.

- **Money**
- **Honey**
- **Abbey**
- **Alley**
- **Money**
- **Key**

Blending

Ask your student to blend the following sounds into words.

- **K-i-d-n-ey**
- **H-o-n-ey**
- **M-o-n-e-y**
- **S-m-i-l-ey**
- **A-l-l-e-y**
- **A-b-b-e-y**

Hear it
Segmenting

Ask your student to break apart the following words into sounds.

- **Honey**
- **Key**
- **Abbey**
- **Money**
- **Alley**
- **Honey**

Rhyming

Read the pair of words. If the two words rhyme, ask students to put a thumb up. If they do not rhyme, ask them to put a thumb down.

- **Money**   **Alley**
- **Honey**   **Honest**
- **Money**   **Honey**

Decode it

Word Reading

Ask your student to read the following words.

- **Volley**
- **Alley**
- **Honey**
- **Kidney**
- **Money**
- **Valley**

Sentence Reading

Ask your student to read the following sentences.

- **The monkey likes to eat.**
- **They eat honey in the alley.**
- **The donkey is very tired.**
- **She went to the valley**

Read it

A bee makes honey in the hive. The honey is sweet. Humans, monkeys, and donkeys all like the gooey honey. The bee hive is in the valley. It is good for all to eat. So humans take honey back home and eat it all day long.

READ IT—THE 5 W'S (OPTIONAL)

Name: _____

Date: _____

Who?	
What?	
When?	
Where?	
Why?	

Read it
Silly Sentences

Ask your student to read the following nonsense words from the box below. Though these are not real words, the goal is to get students to read them fluently and quickly. To accomplish this, you student may try as many times as possible within 3-5 minutes.

1. **The fleys drat by the trey.**
2. **Bey the vey for the zey.**
3. **Wey the geep in the vey.**
4. **Ley the teep on the drey.**
5. **Sey the keet to the dres.**

Spell it

Ask your student to spell and write the following words: Key, Honey, Money, Alley, Abbey.

_____ _____ _____

_____ _____ _____ _____

_____ _____ _____ _____

_____ _____ _____ _____

_____ _____ _____ _____

Spell it
Word Ladder

Find the word at the bottom of the ladder.
Ask your student to change a few letters to make a new word.
For example, "Late" can be changed into "Fate" but changing the
first letter. Ask your student to do this until they run out of
words or complete the ladder.

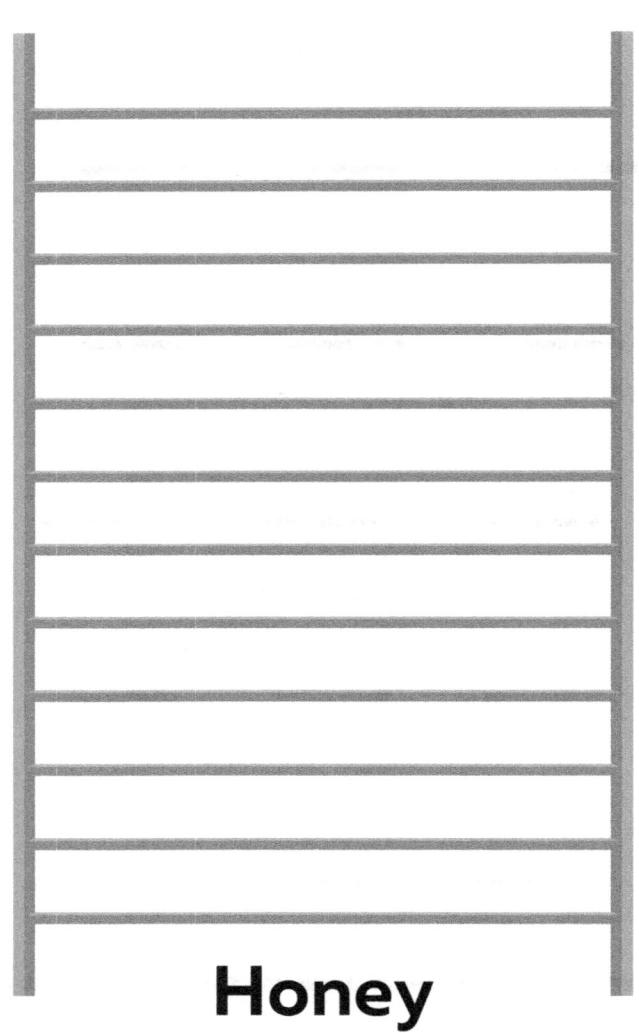

Honey

Long E Vowel Team-ei and ie Set 1

Hear it

Isolating

Ask your student to isolate the **beginning** sound in each word. Do not allow them to see the words or the book. This is an oral exercise.

- **Seize**
- **Weird**
- **Movie**
- **Chief**
- **Yield**
- **Thief**

Ask your student to isolate the **middle** sound in each word. Do not allow them to see the words or the book. This is an oral exercise.

- **Thief**
- **Chief**
- **Brief**
- **This**
- **Chef**
- **Weird**

Hear it

Isolating

Ask your student to isolate the **last** sound in each word. Do not allow them to see the words or the book. This is an oral exercise.

- **Field**
- **Yield**
- **Thief**
- **Grief**
- **Fiend**
- **Movie**

Blending

Ask your student to blend the following sounds into words.

- **B-r-ie-f**
- **M-o-v-ie**
- **G-r-ie-f**
- **Y-ie-l-d**
- **Th-ie-f**
- **S-ei-ze**

117

Hear it

Segmenting

Ask your student to break apart the following words into sounds.

- **Chief**
- **Piece**
- **Niece**
- **Seize**
- **Being**
- **Brief**

Rhyming

Read the pair of words. If the two words rhyme, ask students to put a thumb up. If they do not rhyme, ask them to put a thumb down.

- **Piece**   **Least**
- **Chief**   **Thief**
- **Beige**   **Bingo**

Decode it

Word Reading

Ask your student to read the following words.

- **Chief**
- **Weird**
- **Seize**
- **Field**
- **Yield**
- **Thief**

Sentence Reading

Ask your student to read the following sentences.

- **The chief will have them.**
- **The thief is you!**
- **She sees a piece of cake.**
- **They believe in you!**

Read it

A thief crept into the night. He wore a mask to hide his face. The thief saw a weird pie. He seized a piece and smiled. He tried to tie a bag with his loot. The thief was brief and neat. He believed he was unseen. As he left, he tripped on a rope. The pie fell, and he fled. The thief went back to the field.

READ IT-THE 5 W'S (OPTIONAL)

Name: _____

Date: _____

Who?	
What?	
When?	
Where?	
Why?	

Read it
Silly Sentences

Ask your student to read the following nonsense words from the box below. Though these are not real words, the goal is to get students to read them fluently and quickly. To accomplish this, you student may try as many times as possible within 3-5 minutes.

1. **The peil fies to the wie.**
2. **Neik the seip with deil.**
3. **Veit the liep on the treid.**
4. **Feit the piek by the wein.**
5. **Keil sees the beit near the greil.**

Spell it

Ask your student to spell and write the following words: Chief, Thief, Yield, field, Seize.

Spell it
Word Ladder

Find the word at the bottom of the ladder.
Ask your student to change a few letters to make a new word.
For example, "Late" can be changed into "Fate" but changing the
first letter. Ask your student to do this until they run out of
words or complete the ladder.

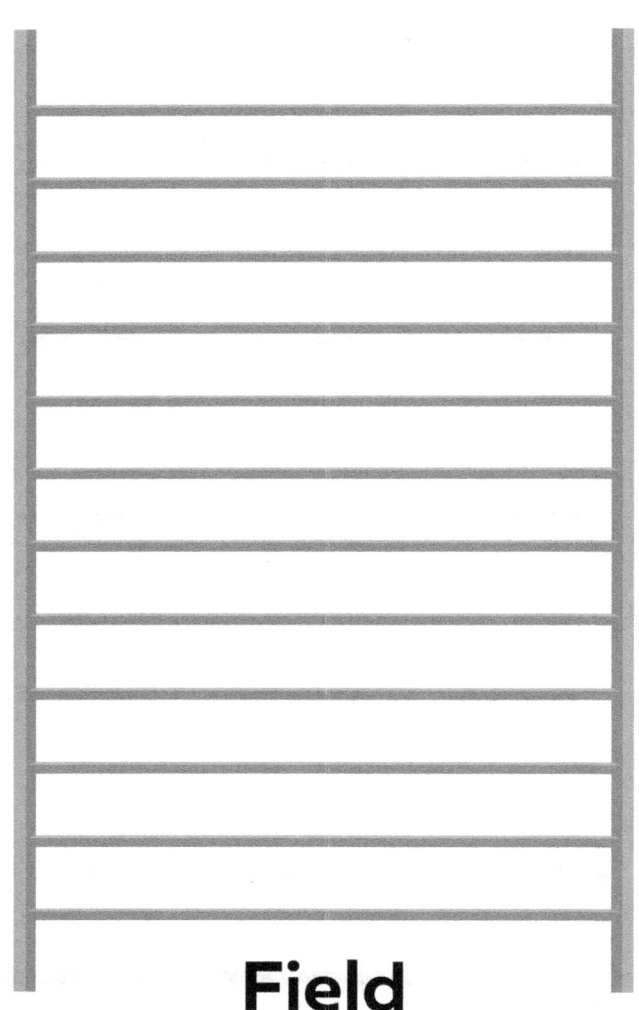

Field

Spell it
Word Ladder

Find the word at the bottom of the ladder.
Ask your student to change a few letters to make a new word.
For example, "Late" can be changed into "Fate" but changing the
first letter. Ask your student to do this until they run out of
words or complete the ladder.

Chief

Long E Vowel Team-ei and ie Set 2

Hear it

Isolating

Ask your student to isolate the **beginning** sound in each word. Do not allow them to see the words or the book. This is an oral exercise.

- **Seize**
- **Belief**
- **Grief**
- **Indie**
- **Field**
- **Brief**

Ask your student to isolate the **middle** sound in each word. Do not allow them to see the words or the book. This is an oral exercise.

- **Bed**
- **Niece**
- **Yield**
- **Belief**
- **Being**
- **Seize**

Hear it

Isolating

Ask your student to isolate the **last** sound in each word. Do not allow them to see the words or the book. This is an oral exercise.

- Chief
- Siege
- Fiend
- Niece
- Piece
- Believe

Blending

Ask your student to blend the following sounds into words.

- G-r-ie-f
- Ch-ie-f
- N-ie-ce
- F-ie-n-d
- P-ie-ce
- S-ei-ze

Hear it

Segmenting

Ask your student to break apart the following words into sounds.

- **Piece**
- **Field**
- **Brief**

- **Beige**
- **Niece**
- **Yield**

Rhyming

Read the pair of words. If the two words rhyme, ask students to put a thumb up. If they do not rhyme, ask them to put a thumb down.

- **Piece**   **Niece**
- **Chief**   **Grief**
- **Brief**   **Bean**

Decode it
Word Reading

Ask your student to read the following words.

- **Diesel**
- **Yield**
- **Thief**
- **Studied**
- **Junkie**
- **Priest**

Sentence Reading

Ask your student to read the following sentences.

- **She studied for her test.**
- **They will seize the rope.**
- **His room is junkie.**
- **We believe in dreams.**

Read it

The girl studied for her test. The test asked the girl to pull a rope. She seized the rope and pulled it close. But the rope did not yield. Then a priest walked by. He helped the girl seize the rope and pull it close. All it took was a brief moment and they had done it. The priest went back to the field and the girl went home.

READ IT—THE 5 W'S (OPTIONAL)

Name: _____

Date: _____

Who?	
What?	
When?	
Where?	
Why?	

Read it
Silly Sentences

Ask your student to read the following nonsense words from the box below. Though these are not real words, the goal is to get students to read them fluently and quickly. To accomplish this, you student may try as many times as possible within 3-5 minutes.

1. **The deil fies the neip.**
2. **Sheip the beit to the weir.**
3. **Geil the piek with lein.**
4. **Heit the teid by the feir.**
5. **Reik the meik on the deif.**

Spell it

Ask your student to spell and write the following words: Priest, Seize, Yield, Field, Grief.

133

Spell it
Word Ladder

Find the word at the bottom of the ladder.
Ask your student to change a few letters to make a new word.
For example, "Late" can be changed into "Fate" but changing the
first letter. Ask your student to do this until they run out of
words or complete the ladder.

Field

Spell it
Word Ladder

Find the word at the bottom of the ladder.
Ask your student to change a few letters to make a new word.
For example, "Late" can be changed into "Fate" but changing the
first letter. Ask your student to do this until they run out of
words or complete the ladder.

Seize

Long I Vowel Team=ie and igh Set 1

Hear it

Isolating

Ask your student to isolate the **beginning** sound in each word. Do not allow them to see the words or the book. This is an oral exercise.

- **Pie**
- **Tie**
- **Lie**
- **Light**
- **Fight**
- **Sight**

Ask your student to isolate the **middle** sound in each word. Do not allow them to see the words or the book. This is an oral exercise.

- **Rid**
- **Tried**
- **Sit**
- **Right**
- **Trip**
- **Sight**

Hear it

Isolating

Ask your student to isolate the **last** sound in each word. Do not allow them to see the words or the book. This is an oral exercise.

- **Tight**
- **Might**
- **High**
- **Fried**
- **Dried**
- **Pie**

Blending

Ask your student to blend the following sounds into words.

- **T-ie**
- **L-ie**
- **P-ie**
- **S-igh-t**
- **F-r-ie-d**
- **M-igh-t**

137

Hear it

Segmenting

Ask your student to break apart the following words into sounds.

- **Light**
- **Cried**
- **Sight**
- **Might**
- **Tried**
- **Tied**

Rhyming

Read the pair of words. If the two words rhyme, ask students to put a thumb up. If they do not rhyme, ask them to put a thumb down.

- **Light**   **Fight**
- **Sight**   **Site**
- **Cried**   **Creed**

Decode it

Word Reading

Ask your student to read the following words.

- **Cried**
- **Tried**
- **Tied**
- **Fried**
- **Dried**
- **Pie**

Sentence Reading

Ask your student to read the following sentences.

- **The light is bright.**
- **He will tie his kite.**
- **The knight rides at night.**
- **She tried a new pie.**

Read it

A boy made a pie with his mom. The pie was high and bright with fruit. He tried to tie a bow around it. The light in the kitchen was warm. At night, they had the pie for a treat. The boy felt delight with each bite. The pie was sweet and neat. They shared the pie with a friend. It was the best pie he ever had.

READ IT—THE 5 W'S (OPTIONAL)

Name: _____

Date: _____

Who?	
What?	
When?	
Where?	
Why?	

Read it
Silly Sentences

Ask your student to read the following nonsense words from the box below. Though these are not real words, the goal is to get students to read them fluently and quickly. To accomplish this, you student may try as many times as possible within 3-5 minutes.

1. **The kigh sees a riet.**
2. **Bligh the miet on the ligh.**
3. **Ries the pligh to the biel.**
4. **Heigh the driet by the siel.**
5. **Riet the brigh with a kleigh.**

Spell it

Ask your student to spell and write the following words: Sigh, High, Might, Sight, Right.

_____ _____ _____ _____

_____ _____ _____ _____

_____ _____ _____ _____ _____

_____ _____ _____ _____ _____

_____ _____ _____ _____ _____

Spell it
Word Ladder

Find the word at the bottom of the ladder.
Ask your student to change a few letters to make a new word.
For example, "Late" can be changed into "Fate" but changing the
first letter. Ask your student to do this until they run out of
words or complete the ladder.

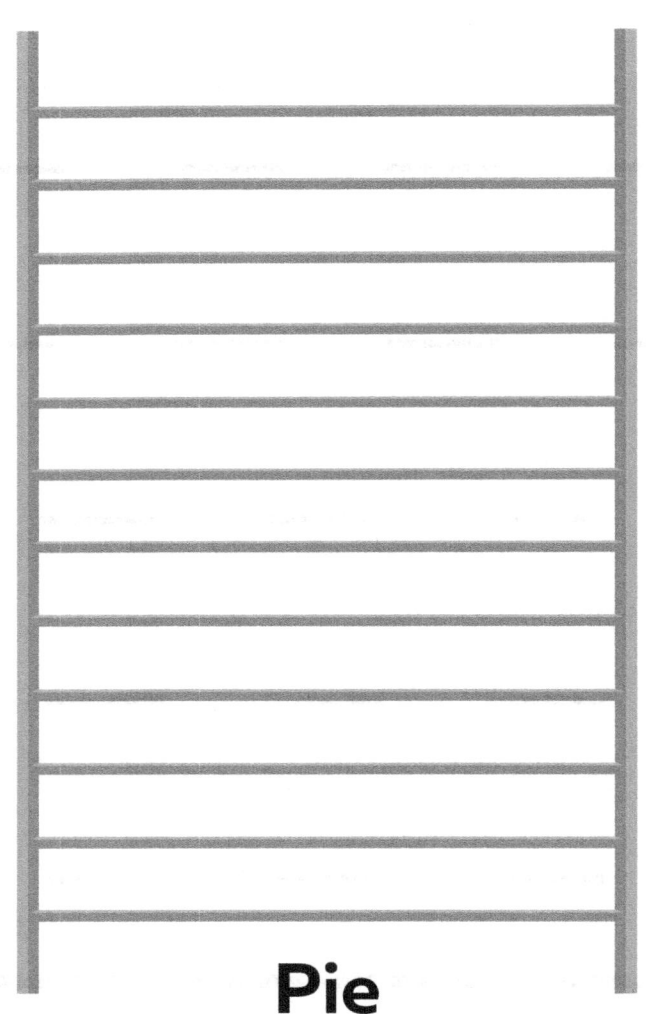

Pie

Spell it
Word Ladder

Find the word at the bottom of the ladder.
Ask your student to change a few letters to make a new word.
For example, "Late" can be changed into "Fate" but changing the
first letter. Ask your student to do this until they run out of
words or complete the ladder.

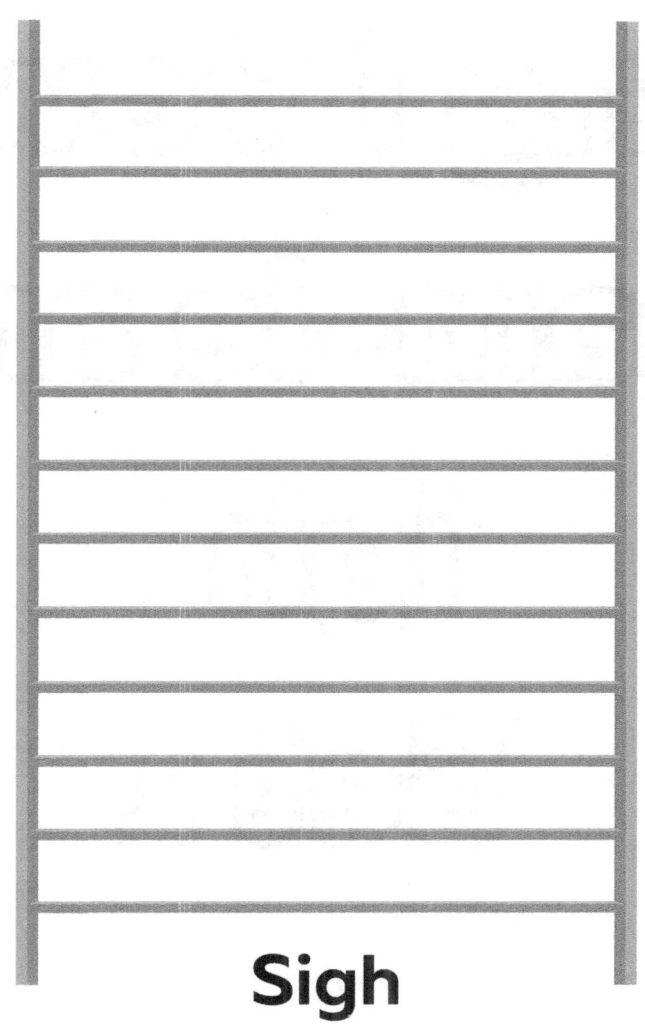

Sigh

Long I Vowel Team-ie and igh Set 1

Hear it

Isolating

Ask your student to isolate the **beginning** sound in each word. Do not allow them to see the words or the book. This is an oral exercise.

- **Ties**
- **Lies**
- **Pies**

- **Right**
- **Sight**
- **Sigh**

Ask your student to isolate the **middle** sound in each word. Do not allow them to see the words or the book. This is an oral exercise.

- **Tid**
- **Light**
- **Sight**

- **Tied**
- **Lit**
- **Sit**

Hear it

Isolating

Ask your student to isolate the **last** sound in each word. Do not allow them to see the words or the book. This is an oral exercise.

- **Dried**
- **Fried**
- **Sight**
- **Fight**
- **High**
- **Light**

Blending

Ask your student to blend the following sounds into words.

- **C-r-ie-d**
- **T-ie-d**
- **T-r-ie-s**
- **F-igh-t**
- **L-igh-t**
- **M-igh-t**

Hear it
Segmenting

Ask your student to break apart the following words into sounds.

- **Cried**
- **Tried**
- **Ties**

- **Might**
- **High**
- **Sigh**

Rhyming

Read the pair of words. If the two words rhyme, ask students to put a thumb up. If they do not rhyme, ask them to put a thumb down.

- **Sigh**   **Hip**
- **Tie**   **Tied**
- **Fight**   **Flight**

148

Decode it

Word Reading

Ask your student to read the following words.

- **Fried**
- **Pie**
- **Tried**
- **Might**
- **Sight**
- **Light**

Sentence Reading

Ask your student to read the following sentences.

- **The sight is bright.**
- **He has tried to tie the rope.**
- **He cried to get the pie.**
- **She played the game with all her might.**

Read it

A boy found dice. It was small and bright. He held it up high and gave a big smile. He wanted to show his friend the sight. They both tried to roll the dice . It took a lot of might. The dice landed on five. They ate a pie too. The day was fun and full. What an amazing sight!

READ IT—THE 5 W'S (OPTIONAL)

Name: _____

Date: _____

Who?	
What?	
When?	
Where?	
Why?	

Read it
Silly Sentences

Ask your student to read the following nonsense words from the box below. Though these are not real words, the goal is to get students to read them fluently and quickly. To accomplish this, you student may try as many times as possible within 3-5 minutes.

1. **The bligh sees a riet.**
2. **Wies the pligh to the biel.**
3. **Tigh the triet by the siel.**
4. **Riet the fligh with a kleigh.**
5. **The brigh ate a deil.**

Spell it

Ask your student to spell and write the following words: Tied, Ties, Right, Fight, Tried.

Spell it
Word Ladder

Find the word at the bottom of the ladder.
Ask your student to change a few letters to make a new word.
For example, "Late" can be changed into "Fate" but changing the
first letter. Ask your student to do this until they run out of
words or complete the ladder.

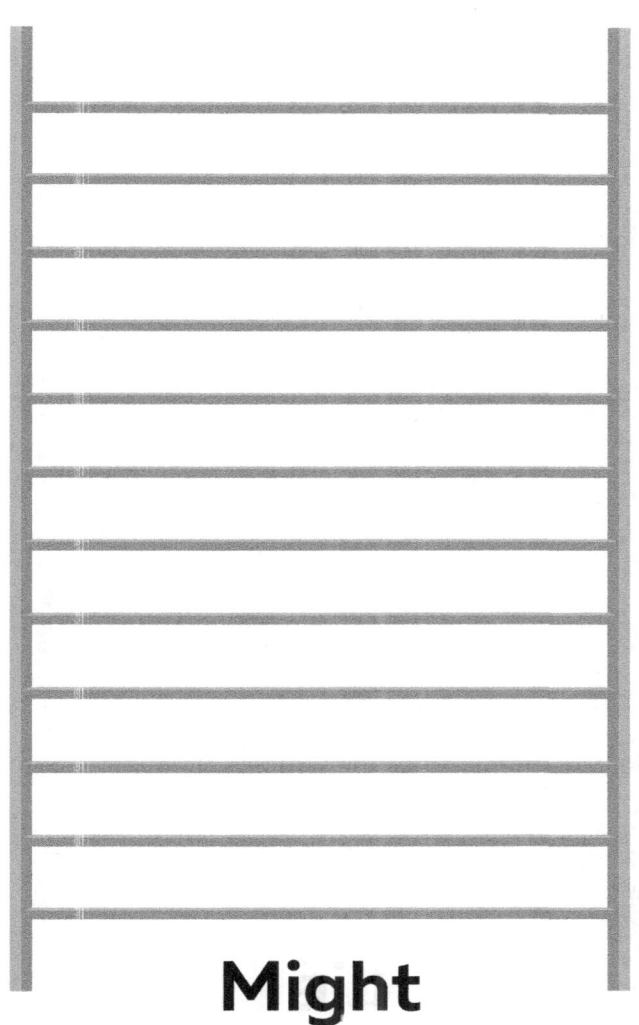

Might

Spell it
Word Ladder

Find the word at the bottom of the ladder.
Ask your student to change a few letters to make a new word.
For example, "Late" can be changed into "Fate" but changing the
first letter. Ask your student to do this until they run out of
words or complete the ladder.

Lie

Long O Vowel Team—oa and oe Set 1

Hear it

Isolating

Ask your student to isolate the **beginning** sound in each word. Do not allow them to see the words or the book. This is an oral exercise.

- **Oak**
- **Oat**
- **Boat**
- **Toe**
- **Foe**
- **Doe**

Ask your student to isolate the **middle** sound in each word. Do not allow them to see the words or the book. This is an oral exercise.

- **Coal**
- **Coat**
- **Foam**
- **Goal**
- **Goat**
- **Load**

Hear it

Isolating

Ask your student to isolate the **last** sound in each word. Do not allow them to see the words or the book. This is an oral exercise.

- **Oak**
- **Foe**
- **Doe**
- **Loaf**
- **Loan**
- **Oath**

Blending

Ask your student to blend the following sounds into words.

- **Oa-k**
- **Oa-t**
- **Oa-th**
- **T-oe**
- **F-oe**
- **D-oe**

Hear it

Segmenting

Ask your student to break apart the following words into sounds.

- **Toast**
- **Foam**
- **Boat**
- **Coal**
- **Toe**
- **Bot**

Rhyming

Read the pair of words. If the two words rhyme, ask students to put a thumb up. If they do not rhyme, ask them to put a thumb down.

- **Foe**   **Toe**
- **Loan**   **Foam**
- **Boat**   **Both**

Decode it

Word Reading

Ask your student to read the following words.

- **Loaf**
- **Loan**
- **Oath**
- **Oak**
- **Oat**
- **Boat**

Sentence Reading

Ask your student to read the following sentences.

- **The boat floats on the lake.**
- **She will toast the bread.**
- **The goat eats green oats.**
- **He had a oak coat.**

Read it

A goat stood by the road. It saw a boat float on the lake. The goat liked to roam and explore. It found an old coat by a tree. The coat had a big hole. The goat tried to eat it but did not like it. It saw a toad and gave it a hit. The goat liked its day by the lake.

READ IT–THE 5 W'S (OPTIONAL)

Name: _____

Date: _____

Who?	
What?	
When?	
Where?	
Why?	

Read it
Silly Sentences

Ask your student to read the following nonsense words from the box below. Though these are not real words, the goal is to get students to read them fluently and quickly. To accomplish this, you student may try as many times as possible within 3-5 minutes.

1. **The toap floats on the loap.**
2. **Zoat the foat by the shoal.**
3. **The goap has a cloap.**
4. **The broat sees a hoab.**
5. **Coes and foes meet by the bloe.**

Spell it

Ask your student to spell and write the following words: Boat, Goat, Coat, Oath, Load

Spell it
Word Ladder

Find the word at the bottom of the ladder.
Ask your student to change a few letters to make a new word.
For example, "Late" can be changed into "Fate" but changing the
first letter. Ask your student to do this until they run out of
words or complete the ladder.

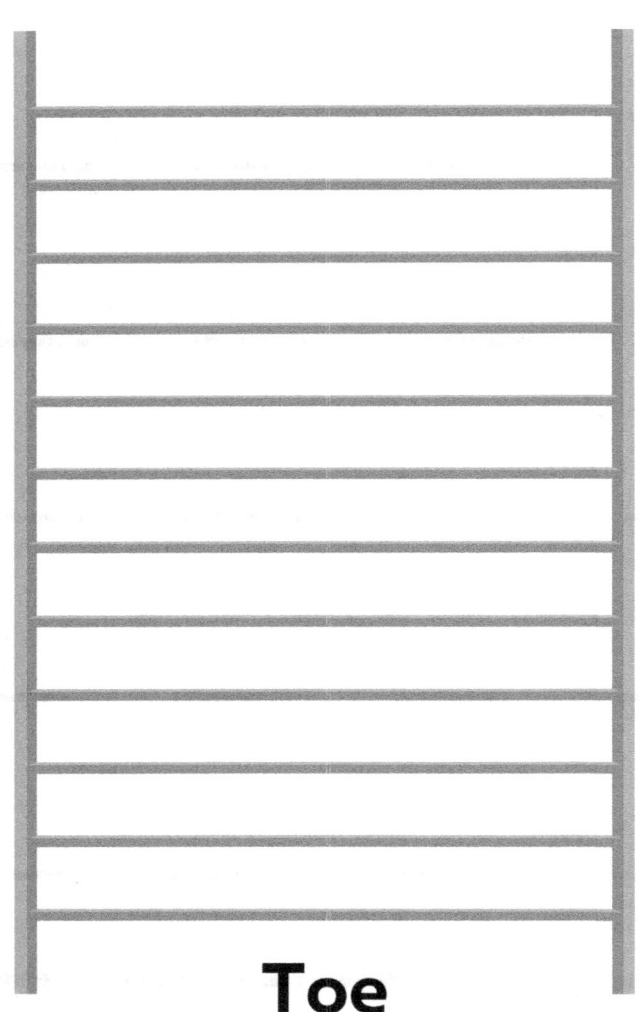

Toe

164

Spell it
Word Ladder

Find the word at the bottom of the ladder.
Ask your student to change a few letters to make a new word.
For example, "Late" can be changed into "Fate" but changing the
first letter. Ask your student to do this until they run out of
words or complete the ladder.

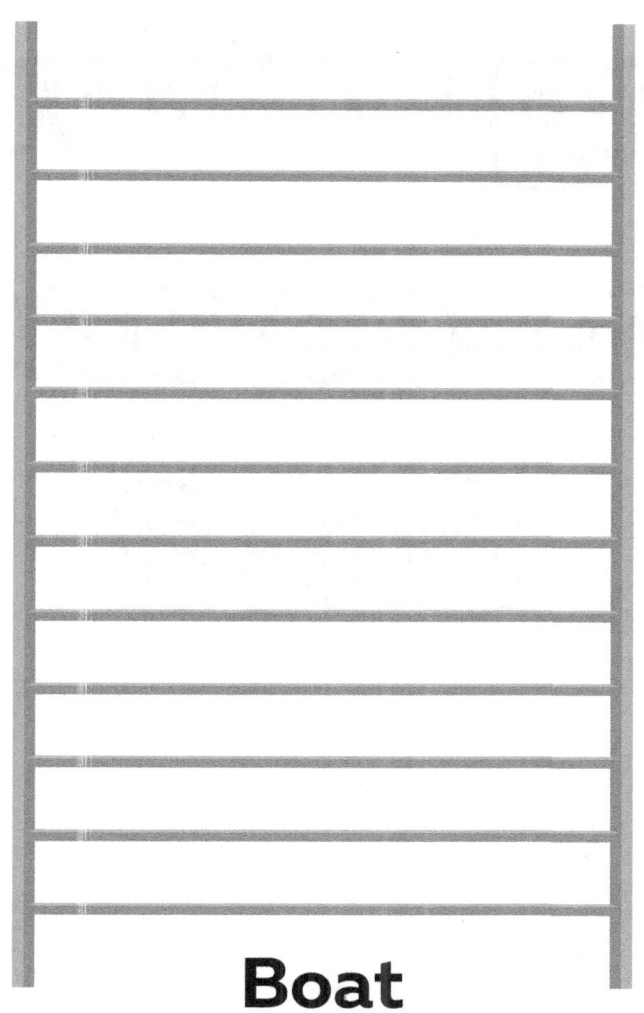

Boat

Long O Vowel Team-oa and oe Set 2

Hear it

Isolating

Ask your student to isolate the **beginning** sound in each word. Do not allow them to see the words or the book. This is an oral exercise.

- **Road**
- **Roam**
- **Soak**
- **Soap**
- **Toad**
- **Bloat**

Ask your student to isolate the **middle** sound in each word. Do not allow them to see the words or the book. This is an oral exercise.

- **Doe**
- **Foal**
- **Toad**
- **Boat**
- **Coat**
- **Coal**

Hear it

Isolating

Ask your student to isolate the **last** sound in each word. Do not allow them to see the words or the book. This is an oral exercise.

- **Cloak**
- **Coach**
- **Coast**
- **Toes**
- **Goes**
- **Toe**

Blending

Ask your student to blend the following sounds into words.

- **F-oa-l**
- **R-oa-m**
- **F-oa-m**
- **S-oa-k**
- **S-oa-p**
- **T-oa-d**

Hear it

Segmenting

Ask your student to break apart the following words into sounds.

- **Float**
- **Toast**
- **Load**

- **Toast**
- **Foe**
- **Toe**

Rhyming

Read the pair of words. If the two words rhyme, ask students to put a thumb up. If they do not rhyme, ask them to put a thumb down.

- **Coat**   **Boat**
- **Load**   **Road**
- **Foe**   **For**

Decode it

Word Reading

Ask your student to read the following words.

- **Cloak**
- **Coach**
- **Coast**
- **Foe**
- **Doe**
- **Road**

Sentence Reading

Ask your student to read the following sentences.

- **The goat crossed the road.**
- **She had a cloak-like coat.**
- **He will float the boat.**
- **The doe stood by the coast.**

Read it

A doe saw a big oak tree by the road. She walked over and saw a toad. The toad croaked and jumped into a boat. The boat began to float away. The doe watched the boat go. She found an old loaf of bread and ate it. As the day went on, the doe felt happy and rested under the oak tree.

READ IT—THE 5 W'S (OPTIONAL)

Name: _____

Date: _____

Who?	
What?	
When?	
Where?	
Why?	

Read it
Silly Sentences

Ask your student to read the following nonsense words from the box below. Though these are not real words, the goal is to get students to read them fluently and quickly. To accomplish this, you student may try as many times as possible within 3-5 minutes.

1. **The roat doats by the bloe.**
2. **Zoap the cloat with a goan.**
3. **The froe voans a sloap.**
4. **Boes and noe zoam the foat.**
5. **The broat roe a gloap.**

Spell it

Ask your student to spell and write the following words: Coal, Goes, Roam, Soak, Soap.

Spell it
Word Ladder

Find the word at the bottom of the ladder.
Ask your student to change a few letters to make a new word.
For example, "Late" can be changed into "Fate" but changing the
first letter. Ask your student to do this until they run out of
words or complete the ladder.

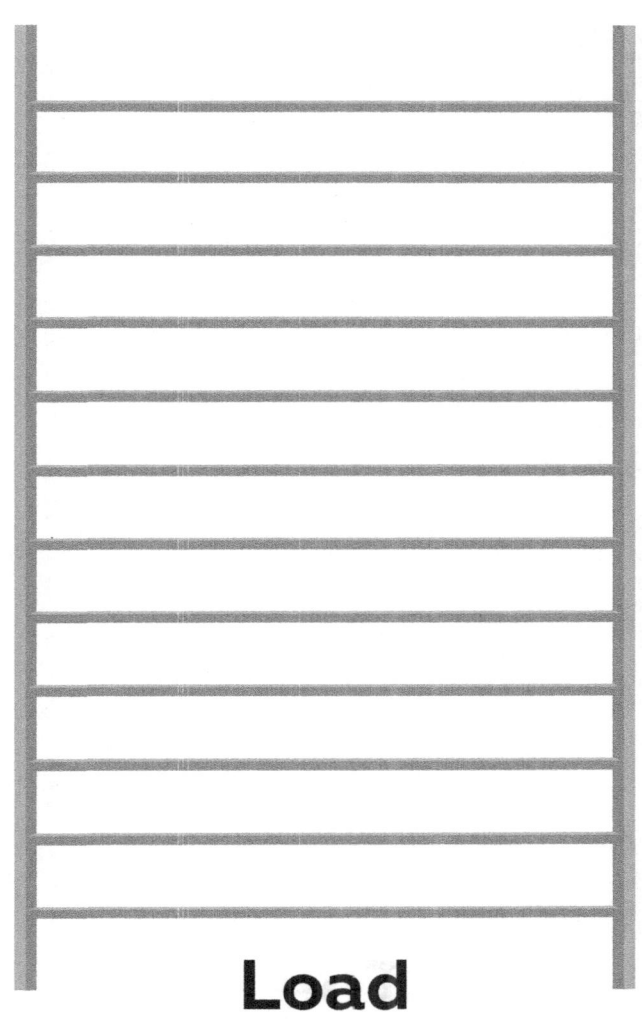

Load

Spell it
Word Ladder

Find the word at the bottom of the ladder.
Ask your student to change a few letters to make a new word.
For example, "Late" can be changed into "Fate" but changing the
first letter. Ask your student to do this until they run out of
words or complete the ladder.

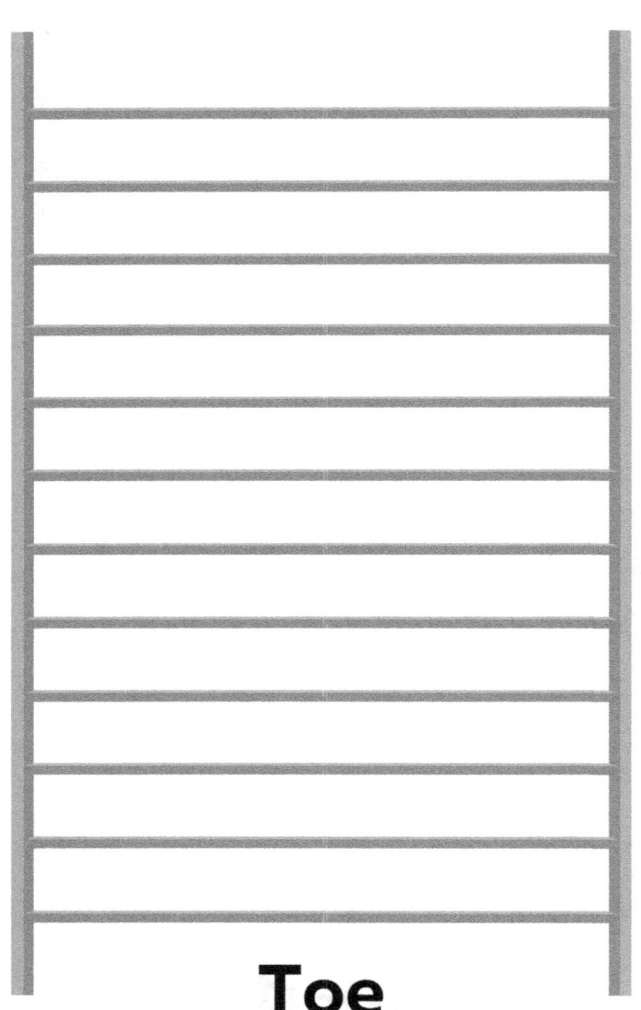

Toe

Long U Vowel Team-ew, ue, eu Set 1

Hear it

Isolating

Ask your student to isolate the **beginning** sound in each word. Do not allow them to see the words or the book. This is an oral exercise.

- **New**
- **Few**
- **Dew**
- **Cue**
- **Rue**
- **Hue**

Ask your student to isolate the **middle** sound in each word. Do not allow them to see the words or the book. This is an oral exercise.

- **Feud**
- **Venue**
- **Sued**
- **Cruel**
- **Gruel**
- **Chewed**

Hear it

Isolating

Ask your student to isolate the **last** sound in each word. Do not allow them to see the words or the book. This is an oral exercise.

- **Cruel**
- **Gruel**
- **Brew**
- **Rescue**
- **Feud**
- **Hues**

Blending

Ask your student to blend the following sounds into words.

- **S-ue**
- **N-ew**
- **F-eu-d**
- **C-ue**
- **S-t-ew**
- **L-ew-i-s**

Hear it

Segmenting

Ask your student to break apart the following words into sounds.

- **Knew**
- **Pew**
- **Chew**
- **Sued**
- **Stew**
- **Dew**

Rhyming

Read the pair of words. If the two words rhyme, ask students to put a thumb up. If they do not rhyme, ask them to put a thumb down.

- **Dew**   **Pew**
- **Sued**   **Cue**
- **Feud**   **Food**

Decode it
Word Reading

Ask your student to read the following words.

- **Cue**
- **Feud**
- **Pew**
- **New**
- **Few**
- **Dew**

Sentence Reading

Ask your student to read the following sentences.

- **The new glue is blue.**
- **She drew a few clues.**
- **Lewis threw food.**
- **They had a feud in the venue.**

Read it

A boy made a stew with new food. He used blue potatoes and a few carrots. He saw a clue in a book about stew. The boy knew the stew needed to simmer. His mom said, "What a great stew!" They all sat down to eat. The stew was a hit, and they had no feud about the taste.

READ IT—THE 5 W'S (OPTIONAL)

Name: _____

Date: _____

Who?	
What?	
When?	
Where?	
Why?	

Read it
Silly Sentences

Ask your student to read the following nonsense words from the box below. Though these are not real words, the goal is to get students to read them fluently and quickly. To accomplish this, you student may try as many times as possible within 3-5 minutes.

1. **The fleu trew to the glew.**
2. **Vew the fue with beus.**
3. **The zeus frew the plew.**
4. **Gue the bleus by the trew.**
5. **Feus and glew make a uew.**

Spell it

Ask your student to spell and write the following words: Stew, Drew, Feud, Knew, Chew.

--- --- --- ---

--- --- --- ---

--- --- --- ---

--- --- --- ---

--- --- --- ---

Spell it
Word Ladder

Find the word at the bottom of the ladder.
Ask your student to change a few letters to make a new word.
For example, "Late" can be changed into "Fate" but changing the
first letter. Ask your student to do this until they run out of
words or complete the ladder.

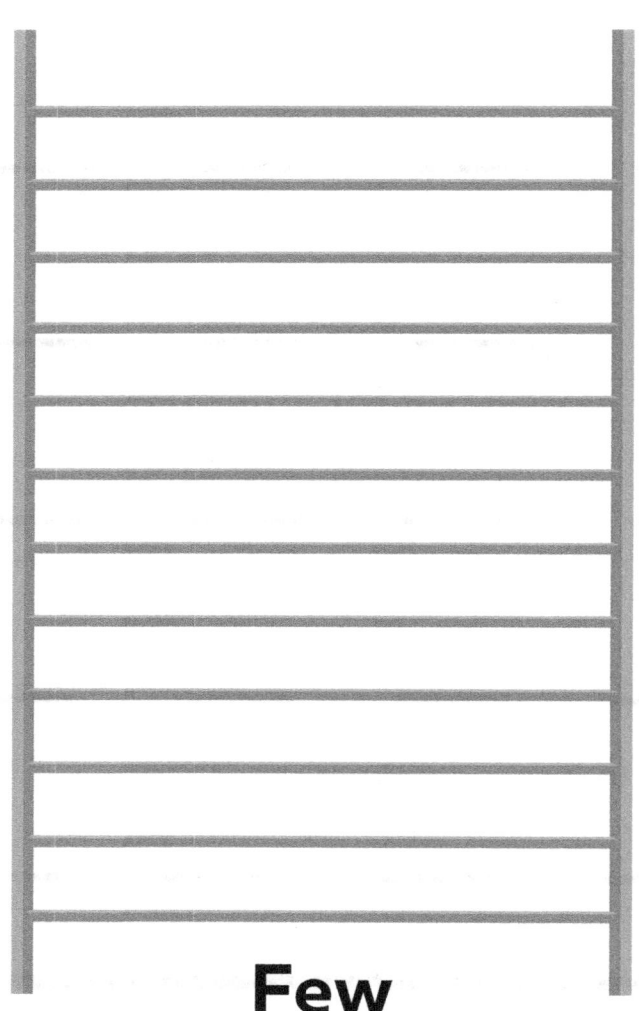

Few

Spell it
Word Ladder

Find the word at the bottom of the ladder.
Ask your student to change a few letters to make a new word.
For example, "Late" can be changed into "Fate" but changing the
first letter. Ask your student to do this until they run out of
words or complete the ladder.

Cue

Spell it
Word Ladder

Find the word at the bottom of the ladder.
Ask your student to change a few letters to make a new word.
For example, "Late" can be changed into "Fate" but changing the
first letter. Ask your student to do this until they run out of
words or complete the ladder.

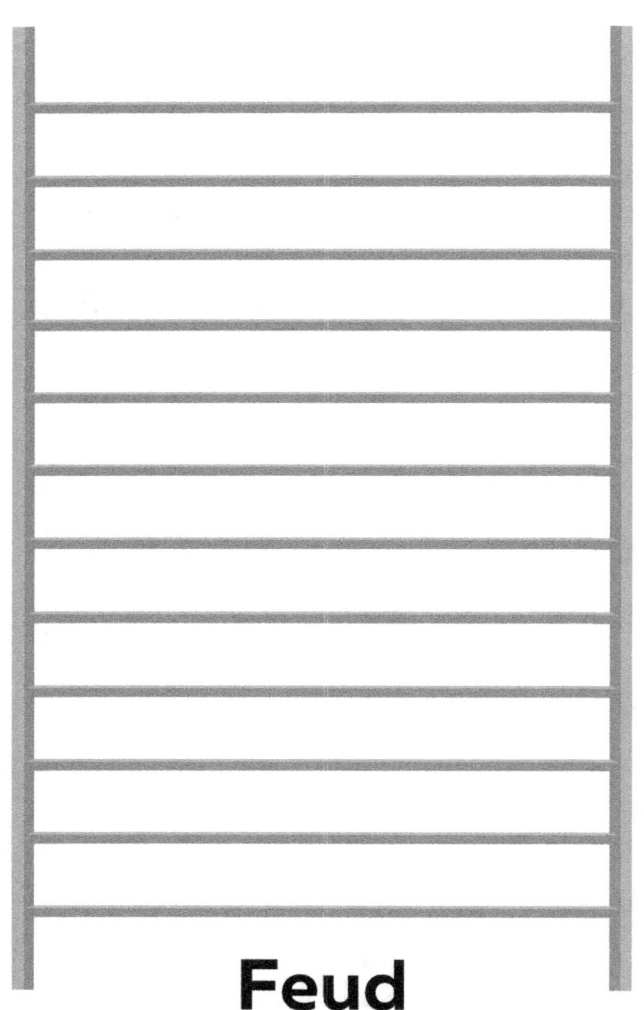

Feud

186

Long U Vowel Team—ew, ue, eu Set 2

Hear it

Isolating

Ask your student to isolate the **beginning** sound in each word. Do not allow them to see the words or the book. This is an oral exercise.

- **Renew**
- **Newbie**
- **View**
- **Value**
- **Crew**
- **Knew**

Ask your student to isolate the **middle** sound in each word. Do not allow them to see the words or the book. This is an oral exercise.

- **Viewed**
- **News**
- **Skews**
- **Blues**
- **Dues**
- **Hues**

Hear it

Isolating

Ask your student to isolate the **last** sound in each word. Do not allow them to see the words or the book. This is an oral exercise.

- **Renew**
- **Undue**
- **Sued**
- **Rue**
- **Newish**
- **Lewis**

Blending

Ask your student to blend the following sounds into words.

- **D-ue**
- **H-ue**
- **L-ew-i-s**
- **V-iew-s**
- **N-ew-s**
- **A-n-ew**

Hear it

Segmenting

Ask your student to break apart the following words into sounds.

- **Argue**
- **Blue**
- **Value**
- **Crew**
- **Askew**
- **Few**

Rhyming

Read the pair of words. If the two words rhyme, ask students to put a thumb up. If they do not rhyme, ask them to put a thumb down.

- **Few**   **Dew**
- **Blue**   **Glue**
- **Sue**   **Sit**

Decode it

Word Reading

Ask your student to read the following words.

- **Rue**
- **Lewis**
- **Skew**
- **Threw**
- **Hue**
- **Venue**

Sentence Reading

Ask your student to read the following sentences.

- **The blue glue is new.**
- **She knew the true clue.**
- **They argue and then renew.**
- **Few people value the venue.**

Read it

A girl had blue glue. She used the glue to fix her toy. The glue was new and very strong. Her friend came over to help. They worked together to give the toys more value. The glue made the toy look like new. Few things are better than fixing toys. The blue glue saved the day for the two friends.

READ IT—THE 5 W'S (OPTIONAL)

Name: _____

Date: _____

Who?	
What?	
When?	
Where?	
Why?	

Read it
Silly Sentences

Ask your student to read the following nonsense words from the box below. Though these are not real words, the goal is to get students to read them fluently and quickly. To accomplish this, you student may try as many times as possible within 3–5 minutes.

1. **The bleu frew freu.**
2. **Geu the plew in the trew.**
3. **Fue the quew by the fleu.**
4. **The sneu kew the dreu.**
5. **Steu the meuw with the que.**

Spell it

Ask your student to spell and write the following words: Glue, View, Anew, Skew, Crew.

--- --- --- ---

--- --- --- ---

--- --- --- ---

--- --- --- ---

--- --- --- ---

194

Spell it
Word Ladder

Find the word at the bottom of the ladder.
Ask your student to change a few letters to make a new word.
For example, "Late" can be changed into "Fate" but changing the
first letter. Ask your student to do this until they run out of
words or complete the ladder.

New

Spell it
Word Ladder

Find the word at the bottom of the ladder.
Ask your student to change a few letters to make a new word.
For example, "Late" can be changed into "Fate" but changing the
first letter. Ask your student to do this until they run out of
words or complete the ladder.

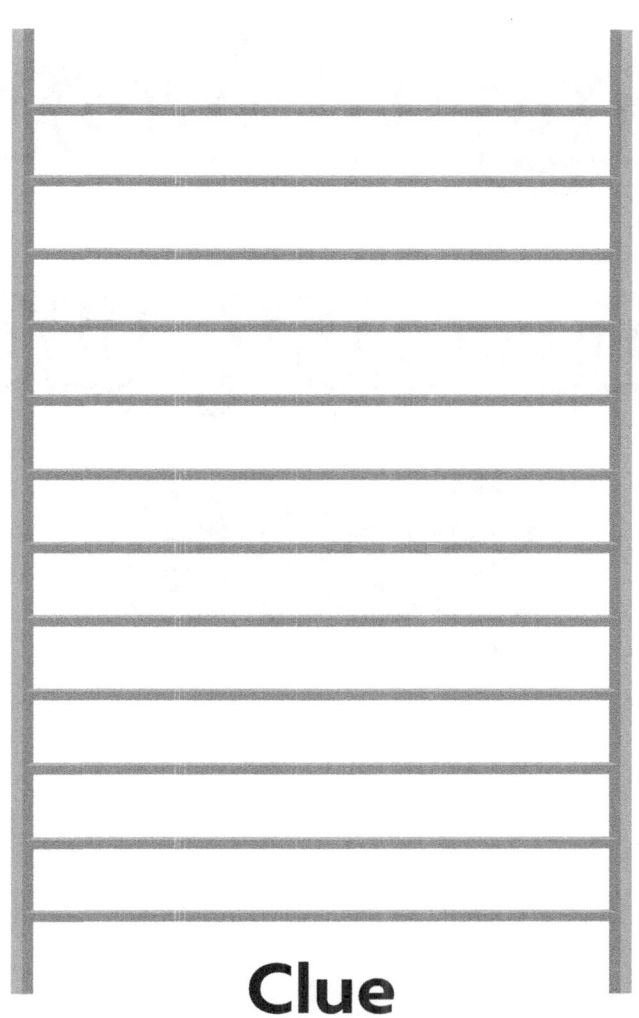

Clue

Long U Vowel Team-ew, ue, eu Set 3

Hear it

Isolating

Ask your student to isolate the **beginning** sound in each word. Do not allow them to see the words or the book. This is an oral exercise.

- **Askew**
- **Crews**
- **jewel**
- **Newly**
- **Renew**
- **Screw**

Ask your student to isolate the **middle** sound in each word. Do not allow them to see the words or the book. This is an oral exercise.

- **Fuel**
- **Clues**
- **Cruel**
- **Viewed**
- **Queued**
- **Deuce**

Hear it

Isolating

Ask your student to isolate the **last** sound in each word. Do not allow them to see the words or the book. This is an oral exercise.

- **Sewer**
- **Shrew**
- **Sinew**
- **Jewel**
- **Neuro**
- **Ensue**

Blending

Ask your student to blend the following sounds into words.

- **C-l-ue**
- **E-n-s-ue**
- **Sh-r-ew**
- **N-eu-r-o**
- **Eu-r-o**
- **S-ew-er**

Hear it

Segmenting

Ask your student to break apart the following words into sounds.

- **Flew**
- **Drew**
- **Issue**
- **Queue**
- **Stew**
- **Clue**

Rhyming

Read the pair of words. If the two words rhyme, ask students to put a thumb up. If they do not rhyme, ask them to put a thumb down.

- **Clue**   **Blue**
- **Drew**   **Crew**
- **Flew**   **Flue**

Decode it

Word Reading

Ask your student to read the following words.

- **Value**
- **Stew**
- **Crew**
- **Newly**
- **Renew**
- **Untrue**

Sentence Reading

Ask your student to read the following sentences.

- **She threw the gum in the stew.**
- **He has a blue brew.**
- **His mum said it was untrue.**
- **They had to wait on a queue**

Read it

The crew had a new task. They needed to build a blue boat. They used glue to join the wood. Each crew member knew their job well. The sun was bright, and they worked fast. The boat began to have value. Few things made them as proud as this.Their hard work and glue made it strong.

READ IT—THE 5 W'S (OPTIONAL)

Name: _____

Date: _____

Who?	
What?	
When?	
Where?	
Why?	

Read it
Silly Sentences

Ask your student to read the following nonsense words from the box below. Though these are not real words, the goal is to get students to read them fluently and quickly. To accomplish this, you student may try as many times as possible within 3-5 minutes.

1. **The dreu feuw by a fleu.**
2. **Steu the feur peu.**
3. **Lew and feu kew the kew.**
4. **The fleu teu the pue**
5. **Quew the few peu.**

Spell it

Ask your student to spell and write the following words: Shrew, Threw, Queue, Askew, Glued.

Spell it
Word Ladder

Find the word at the bottom of the ladder.
Ask your student to change a few letters to make a new word.
For example, "Late" can be changed into "Fate" but changing the
first letter. Ask your student to do this until they run out of
words or complete the ladder.

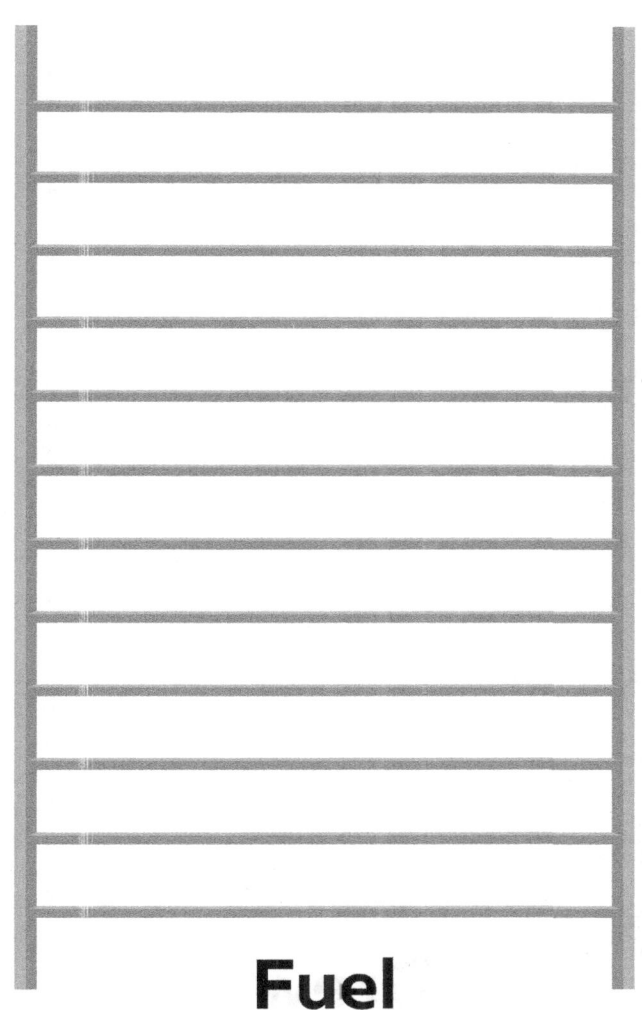

Fuel

Spell it
Word Ladder

Find the word at the bottom of the ladder.
Ask your student to change a few letters to make a new word.
For example, "Late" can be changed into "Fate" but changing the
first letter. Ask your student to do this until they run out of
words or complete the ladder.

Drew

Blank Lesson Plan Template

Dear Readers,

Thank you so much for completing "The Science of Reading Decodable Curriculum"! We are thrilled that you have taken this important step in your child's reading journey. Your dedication and hard work are making a big difference.

As a special bonus, we are excited to introduce our blank lesson plan template. This template is designed to help you reteach any sounds that your child might need extra practice with. You can also use it to introduce new sounds that your child hasn't learned yet. The template follows the same format as the lessons in the book, making it easy for you to continue supporting your child's learning.

We also want to offer you even more free resources to help with your child's reading journey. If you're interested, please email us and we'll be happy to provide additional materials.

Thank you again for your commitment to your child's education. Keep up the great work!

Adam Free
decodabletexts@gmail.com

Hear it

Isolating

Ask your student to isolate the **blended** sound in each word. Do not allow them to see the words or the book. This is an oral exercise.

- _____
- _____
- _____

- _____
- _____
- _____

Ask your student to isolate the **middle** sound in each word. Do not allow them to see the words or the book. This is an oral exercise.

- _____
- _____
- _____

- _____
- _____
- _____

209

Hear it

Isolating

Ask your student to isolate the **last** sound in each word. Do not allow them to see the words or the book. This is an oral exercise.

- _____
- _____
- _____

- _____
- _____
- _____

Rhyming

Read the pair of words. If the two words rhyme, ask students to put a thumb up. If they do not rhyme, ask them to put a thumb down.

- _____
- _____
- _____

- _____
- _____
- _____

Hear it
Blending

Ask your student to blend the following sounds into words.

- _____
- _____
- _____

- _____
- _____
- _____

Segmenting

Ask your student to break apart the following words into sounds.

- _____
- _____
- _____

- _____
- _____
- _____

Decode it
Word Reading

Ask your student to read the following words.

- _____
- _____
- _____

- _____
- _____
- _____

Sentence Reading

Ask your student to read the following sentences.

- _____
- _____
- _____

Read it

READ IT—THE 5 W'S (OPTIONAL)

Name: _____

Date: _____

Who?	
What?	
When?	
Where?	
Why?	

214

Read it
Silly Sentences

Ask your student to read the following nonsense words from the box below. Though these are not real words, the goal is to get students to read them fluently and quickly. To accomplish this, you student may try as many times as possible within 3-5 minutes.

Spell it

Ask your student to spell and write the following words:

_____ _____ _____ _____ _____

_____ _____ _____ _____ _____

_____ _____ _____ _____ _____

_____ _____ _____ _____ _____

_____ _____ _____ _____ _____

Spell it

Ask your student to write the word in the middle of the page on a white board. Then ask them to change the word into another word, making as few changes as possible. This will likely involve changing only one or two letters. Do not let them see this book while completing this exercise. Ex. Change "mat" into "cat". Change "cat" into "pat". Change "pat" into "pan". Change "pan" into "pad" Etc.

Thank You

Congratulations to all the parents and teachers who have successfully completed this volume of our decodable curriculum! Your dedication and commitment to guiding young readers through this essential phase of their literacy development are truly commendable. By completing this book, you have laid a solid foundation for building strong and confident readers, equipped with the necessary phonemic awareness, phonics, and decoding skills to tackle more complex texts with ease. Your efforts have undoubtedly set the stage for a future filled with academic success and a lifelong love for reading.

As you celebrate this milestone achievement, we encourage you to look forward to the journey ahead with excitement and anticipation. The next book of our curriculum promises to delve deeper into the intricacies of literacy instruction, further enhancing your child's reading abilities and nurturing their passion for learning. Together, let us continue to empower our young readers, providing them with the tools and support they need to thrive in an ever-changing world. Thank you for your unwavering commitment to the success of your children and students. We cannot wait to see the incredible progress they will continue to make in book two and beyond.

CERTIFICATE

OF COMPLETION

This Certificate is proudly presented to

_____

For mastering _____

PRESENTED BY

_____

Made in the USA
Las Vegas, NV
29 November 2024